MEDITATIONS FOR TRANQUILLITY

A PRACTICAL GUIDE TO SPIRITUAL FIRST AID

MEDITATIONS FOR TRANQUILLITY

A PRACTICAL GUIDE TO SPIRITUAL FIRST AID

SUZANNE MARBROOK

CASSELL&CO

First published in the United Kingdom in 2000 by Cassell & Co

A CIP catalogue record for this book is available from the British Library

ISBN 0 304 35588 7

Designed by Richard Carr
Colour separation by Tenon & Polert Colour Scanning Ltd
Printed and bound in Hong Kong by Colorcraft Ltd

Cassell & Co
The Orion Publishing Group
Wellington House
125 Strand
London WC2R 0BB

DEDICATED WITH LOVE

TO MY MOTHER AND FATHER
ANNE AND BEN MARBROOK IN SPIRIT,

TO MY SONS BEN AND SAM MAHAYNI
TO MIRANDA
AND TO SEEKERS OF TRUTH EVERYWHERE.

Contents

Introduction

THE NINETEENTH-CENTURY German philosopher Goethe said: 'Just trust yourself, and you will know how to live.' The twentieth century saw a loss of personal trust with the decline of spiritual autonomy. Generations ago, our ancestors knew how to communicate with nature, and they understood how to see and talk to the spirit world, to gain guidance on mundane and spiritual affairs. They also knew how to utilize the subtle energies flowing through our bodies and through the entire universe.

Psychic abilities and the sixth sense, as it was known, have always been vital for survival and mental health. These most precious abilities were denigrated into virtual obscurity in the western world. Through my work as a holistic healer and a fellow traveller on life's path, I have come to believe that in the twenty-first century personal spiritual renaissance is one of our most pressing needs.

Modern science and computer technology have provided visual evidence to help with an understanding of the ancient wisdom and knowledge. In the 1930s, Kirlian photography revealed a subtle energy field that emanated from all living things. Experiments photographing the human hand demonstrated that the energy field changed with differing mood and energy levels of the physical mind and body. In addition, modern science and quantum theory has confirmed a 'holistic worldview' in which everything is formed of interconnecting energy, with nothing existing in isolation.

We now know that inner tranquillity, good health and spiritual enlightenment rely upon balance, whereby all our subtle energies resonate in harmony with each other and the natural rhythms of the universe. With that in mind, *Meditations for Tranquillity* is designed to be an enjoyable meditative experience, and also extremely helpful in clarifying and integrating the mind, body and spirit towards reaching the highest vibrations for living in the light by regaining and practising our lost abilities.

Radiant good health and spiritual awareness generally coincide with positive calm and inner peace. Though most people would aspire to such a state, it can often be hard-won. Meditation seems to be a key factor in advancing many people's progress.

Individual journeys are unique and have a soul blueprint. Within this personal blueprint we have every choice to work towards reaching our potential, not only to our own benefit but also to the benefit of the universe as a whole.

The twenty-five meditations in this book evolved out of my own ongoing spiritual quest and work as a holistic healer. Shortly after studying non-directive hypnotherapy at the Esalen Institute, California, I started to express through painting my sense of the power and vibrations of colour and form, which deeply affect our lives – particularly the spiritual aspects. The illustrations come not from an intellectual expression but rather from balance and focus, which I believe is the result of working on the integration of mind, body and spirit. The illustrations and the written words all come from the same source, so there is no divergence in placing them together.

May *Meditations for Tranquillity* help you to recognize and trust in your own strengths and to witness your reality in the light of truth.

Miracles are not contrary to nature, they are only contrary to what (we think) we know about nature.

(St Augustine, AD 353)

AN INVITATION

Meditations for Tranquillity is an invitation to work towards your own spiritual enlightenment, by being in charge of all aspects of your life and accepting responsibility for the outcome of your actions.

The meditations will challenge you to explore your core beliefs and personal reality, and to align them with your soul's integrity, the key to living your truth.

Through understanding and empowerment of your own mental, physical and spiritual energies, you will come to 'know' the interconnection of all living things, and your individual contribution through your soul's purpose.

There is no absolute truth, no-one has all the answers. *Meditations for Tranquillity* is designed to act as the touchstone to your soul's integrity and purpose of being.

Prepare to be surprised. In the mean time, the author's blessing.

Train hard, fight easy, and above all enjoy.

PRACTICALITIES AND PRINCIPLES OF MEDITATION

LIFE'S JOURNEY

Life's journey, with no visible destination,
free will to engender doubt and desperation.
No purpose mentioned in the terms of life,
unpublished manuals to assuage concerns and strife.

Precious moments of quiet reflection,
thoughts and daydreams of spiritual perfection.
Truth revealed in shards of fleeting light,
tantalizing glimpses of Eternity in sight.

The State of Tranquillity

*T*HE STATE OF TRANQUILLITY has been eulogized by poets, artists, musicians and philosophers down the ages. This much sought-after state seems to be more needed, and paradoxically more elusive, in contemporary living.

At first glance, tranquillity would appear to be a passive affair, somewhat removed from day-to-day life; but serious seekers have discovered quite the opposite to be true. Many find it to be a fascinating journey of self-discovery and enlightenment.

Milarepa, an illustrious twelfth-century Tibetan Buddhist monk, wrote of his experience: 'This state of tranquillity is maintained by means of continual attention and awareness, not allowing it to become distracted or sink into passivity. Intensified by the force of awareness, one experiences pure consciousness without differentiation, naked, vivid and crisp. These are the characteristics of tranquillity of mind.'

PURE CONSCIOUSNESS

Using the 'holistic worldview' of the interconnectedness of all living things through their energy vibrations, the 25 meditations in this book seek to arrive at pure consciousness by the integration of the mental, physical, astral and spiritual aspects of being. This is with recognition of the synergy between the multi-dimensional aspects of human beings and the vital importance of their harmony.

Essential to this process of integration is the balance and alignment of the left and right hemispheres of the brain, for expression of full expanded consciousness. Also essential is balance and alignment of the chakras and auric energy field, which interface between our mind, physical body and the spiritual self. In pure consciousness, channels open to connect with the higher realms of cosmic consciousness.

The most beautiful experience we can have is the mysterious. He to whom this emotion is a stranger, who can no longer pause to wonder and stand rapt in awe, is as good as dead.

(Albert Einstein)

The 25 meditations represent a personal journey of balance, healing and discovery, starting the journey at the base chakra with the life force of nature and progressing through to the crown chakra, with its connection to the spiritual realms and beyond.

For the past ten years or so, new cosmic energy rays of a higher frequency of light have been entering the earth's atmosphere. Learning to resonate in harmony with these new energies presents opportunities further to raise our own vibration levels for living in the light, and reaching personal potential.

Form, Colour and Concepts

USING THE POWERFUL vibrations of form, colour and concepts, the meditations in this book are intended to centre and focus thought, assisting the reader with a clarity and definition in perception of personal reality and core beliefs.

During the altered state of meditation the conscious mind is resting. Through sharpened awareness, guidance and information is made accessible from the higher self and the higher realms of consciousness.

FORM

Form has been considered of great significance in mysticism and the creative arts for thousands of years. The golden mean ratios in circles, spirals and equilateral triangles are to be seen in Renaissance art, in sacred architecture and megalithic sites such as Stonehenge and the Egyptian pyramids.

The aesthetic qualities of these forms are sacred geometry, which is programmed within us. We are able to recognize sacred geometry which is related to number, pure mathematics and pure sound. Higher astral realms of light and bliss, the form in objects such as crystals, jewels and metal, remind us of 'home' in the spiritual sense.

When day-dreaming or meditating, it is possible to experience *déjà vu* and a sense of excitement and desire to return 'home' when recognition of these forms are triggered within us. The collective creative energy which is also the thread of evolution is also available to us via our own higher self and our own creativity.

The forms in the pictures accompanying the meditations represent the harmonic flux of energy in the continuous process of change. They assist the mind to expand beyond the mundane world of the five senses and the auric energy field, to resonate with the rhythms of the cosmic realms and beyond.

COLOUR

Colour deprivation and the significance of the different colour vibrations on our health and psyche have been well documented. Hospitals have adopted more restful and healing colours for their environments, and it is known that people who are incarcerated in areas which have little or no colour, especially no view of the sky, are prone to suffer a deterioration in mental and physical health.

The ancient alchemists observed that we are surrounded by colours, which we are unable to see and are largely unaware of. The beneficial effects of colours were understood in the ancient practice of Feng Shui in which their characteristics were utilized to create environments conducive to health and tranquillity. The art of colour therapy goes back to the healing temples of light and colour at Heliololis in Egypt; these were also known in China and India.

All life is energy, and colour is one aspect of the differentiation of energy patterns which we can use to our advantage. Today's complementary therapies acknowledge the positive effect that colours can have on consciousness, the physical body, creativity and all aspects of being.

The chakras (see page 26) are represented by the spectrum of the seven rays of colour – red, orange, yellow, green, blue, indigo and violet. All of these are contained within white light. The seven colours have differing wavelengths, qualities and characteristics which are linked to the chakras and resonate with them. Red is the longest wavelength, being nearer to the energy of physical matter. Violet, at the other end of the spectrum, is the shortest, and closer to the mental and spiritual energies. Balance of the movement of the energies within the chakras is considered fundamental to perfect harmony within emotions, mind and spirit and to connecting to the multi-dimensional universe.

Each colour has its own characteristics:

Red – revitalizes the physical body, stimulating the life force, the nervous system and creativity.

Orange – calms and stabilizes emotions, affects circulation and assimilation of oxygen through the lungs and blood-stream.

Yellow – radiates optimism and stimulates the mind; it also has a beneficial effect on the digestive system.

Green – relaxes the body, cools the blood. It is associated with the higher mental body and emotions affecting love and compassion.

Blue – affects self-expression of inner feelings and ideas, and psychic abilities such as clairaudience and clairvoyance.

Indigo – is connected to vision, offering an opportunity for clear perception, affecting insight, integrity and the understanding of life.

Violet – has its connections with the highest elements of human nature, states of total awareness, and of the higher mind and spirituality.

To give an example, Richard had moved into a new home, a flat overlooking the river Thames. After a few weeks his initial euphoria was eclipsed by nervy and irritable feelings, and he realized that he had a deprivation of green – it was midwinter in a city centre, with grey skies and a grey river. Plenty of green indoor plants in the flat, and colour meditations (see page 31) soon restored Richard's balance.

Colours are absorbed into our systems quite naturally, but we can also breathe in the colours during the meditation, and they can be directed to any discomfort or illness within the mind or body. Through visualization the energy of the colour can be used to free blockages, and with the mind focused on the area of illness ask: 'What is the cause of this illness, what are you telling me?' The answer may come immediately or later through dreams or knowing.

Generally speaking, colour directly influences the soul. Colour is the keyboard, the eyes are the hammers, the soul is the piano with many strings. The artist is the hand that plays, touching one key after another persuasively, to cause vibrations in the soul. It is evident therefore that colour harmony must rest ultimately purposely playing upon the human soul; this is one of the guiding principles of internal necessity.

(Wassily Kandinsky, Russian abstract painter)

CONCEPTS

The concepts accompanying each picture in the meditations represent ideas for contemplation. Each is intended to assist in bringing clarity and definition to the reader's perception of personal reality, and core beliefs in relation to the universal oneness. The meditations represent a journey of self-discovery towards enlightenment through awareness.

Even though the journey starts at the base chakra with the life-force energies of nature, and travels through to the crown chakra with its connections to the cosmic energies, the individual chakras are not named, as there is a constant interplay between all the chakras; for example, making a complex decision may involve input of all the chakras.

Initially, it is recommended that the meditations are done in sequence, thereafter by personal preference depending upon moods, energy levels and emotional needs.

The authenticity of any concepts or ideas, and the conclusions which we reach when meditating or contemplating, should always be assessed against our integrity – our own personal standard of judgement. If what is happening in the mind does not resonate in harmony with our integrity, feelings of discomfort and a deep sense of insecurity can follow.

The soul has a blueprint for this life; within it are the potentials and unique characteristics of the individual, one of which is the soul's integrity, linked to the state of 'wholeness' within the mental, physical, emotional and spiritual aspect of being.

Meditation and Yoga

ILAREPA, THE TWELFTH-CENTURY Tibetan Buddhist monk, described meditation as a foundational act of spiritual effort, stating: 'In meditation man seeks to establish a relationship between the sense of self and consciousness, which is its root and foundation.'

Since earliest times, people of all cultures have used the altered states of meditation to commune with the higher self and higher states of consciousness, seeking to rise above the mundane world in search of tranquillity, inspiration and enlightenment. Poet Alfred Lord Tennyson found that 'this heightened or widened state of consciousness gives insight into another level of existence'.

It would seem that inspiration and creativity are deeply dependent on these heightened states of consciousness. Mozart spoke of concentrating his mind on a point of brilliant white light when composing his music. He was one of the few great musicians whose music required no revision.

During meditation and hypnosis, the brain-waves are in the Alpha state of deep relaxation (see page 000). Research has shown that during meditation the left rational part of the brain rests in the Alpha state, and the brain activity shifts to the right hemisphere, with its characteristics of intuitive, abstract, mystical and holistic perceptions of the universe. It was also observed that meditational states were instrumental in restoring balance to the two hemispheres of the brain,

which is considered essential to the 'wholeness of the human being'.

TRANSFORMATION

Fundamental spiritual transformation and liberation usually follows a deeper knowing and understanding of self. During the altered states of meditation, we are able to discern between our actions which have their origins in the memory, having become responses through habit and routine, and actions which have been inspired by the integrity and wisdom of the soul. The latter generate inner calm and tranquillity, through the elimination of conflict between our actions and our soul's integrity.

The 25 meditations help to expand consciousness by reflecting on the authenticity of actions and beliefs, identifying their origin in a detached way, and at the same time assessing how comfortably they sit within the soul's integrity.

SACRED SOUNDS AND SYMBOLS

For thousands of years, mystics and sages of all cultures have understood the valuable characteristics of the sounds and symbols of sacred geometry for meditation. Ernst Chladni, an eighteenth-century German physicist, discovered that sand scattered on stationary steel discs was affected by various notes he played on a violin. The sound frequency moved the sand particles to produce highly organized patterns like mandalas (see below), which are at the heart of nature. Musical instruments such as the piano and violin resonate in sympathy with notes played on other instruments and other sounds within the environment.

The vibrations of the Hindu 'OM' sound spoken aloud or in the mind can balance and tone up the mental and physical body. Sacred geometrical symbols such as the equilateral cross enclosed within a circle (see page 51) and meditational mandalas are all known to have characteristics which, through their vibrations, can bring order and balance to physical matter and to the human consciousness, restoring health at the physical level, and transporting consciousness into ever deeper realms of understanding.

Figure 1 shows a Buddhist 'yantra' or mandala. Most mandalas incorporate a combination of circles, triangles and squares and act as a focus for deep meditation. This example depicts diminishing harmonics. When meditating upon it and moving consciousness to its centre, deeper levels of understanding can be reached with communion to the Cosmic Consciousness

Fig 1: A Typical Buddhist yantra or mandala.

MEDITATION AND VISUALIZATION

The understanding of the left and right brain's activity has been used to develop many effective therapeutic techniques in healing, which are now widely used in stress management and other physiological and psychological illnesses. Meditation, mind control and active visualization techniques utilize the deep relaxed state of meditation, and combine it with the creative and intuitive characteristics of the right brain.

YOGA

Yogis of Tibet and Nepal have demonstrated the efficacy of meditation and mind control, surviving for many years in sub-zero temperatures in the highest mountains, with no external heating and meagre supplies of food. Through advanced meditation techniques, the yogis were able to control skin temperature, heart activity and blood flow.

The following six yoga postures (see Figure 2) have been chosen for their effectiveness in alleviating tension and stress, and focusing the mind. If you are new to the practice of yoga, please take note of these important guidelines. Only do the

exercises if you are physically fit. The postures should never feel stressed or uncomfortable. Wait for at least one hour after eating and, as with all exercise, warm up the body first either by gentle movements or by taking a shower. The aim of the six yoga postures is a reduction of tension and stress by relaxing the mind and body, and generating the natural flow of energy throughout the system.

THE LYING DOG STRETCH
(Figure 2a)
This is one of the most relaxing and simple of all the yoga poses. Sit upright with your hips on your heels and take a few deep breaths; then, while gently bending your body forward, stretch your arms out, letting them lie flat in front of you; resting your head on the floor, breathing normally, stay in this position for a few minutes.

THE CAT
(Figure 2b)
The cat pose releases tension in the back, shoulder and neck areas; it mimics a cat taking a leisurely stretch. Adopt the pose in the illustration, keeping your hands directly underneath

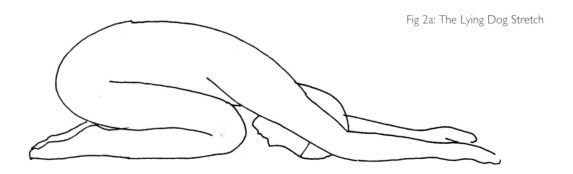

Fig 2a: The Lying Dog Stretch

Fig 2b: The Cat

your shoulders, thighs slightly apart and vertical to the floor. Take a few deep breaths. Keeping your back flat and your neck parallel to the floor, on the in-breath lift your head and slowly hollow your spine, and hold for a few seconds. On the out-breath, slowly arch your spine upwards, bringing your head down again, moving your head towards your chest. Repeat the exercise five or so times, breathing normally and being aware of the timing.

THE RABBIT
(Figure 2c)

The rabbit pose is simple and relaxing. Sit with your hips on your heels and take a few deep

breaths. Invert your spine and roll onto your head, keeping your hands under your shoulders. Breathing normally, hold the pose for ten seconds, or for as long as you feel comfortable.

THE POSE OF TRANQUILLITY
(Figure 2d)

Lie flat on your back with your arms by your side and take a few deep breaths to relax. Then, gently on the in-breath, keeping your arms on the floor for support, swing your legs and hips off the floor and lower them over your head to the same angle as shown in the illustration. When you feel a point of balance, remove your arms from the floor, and hold your shins or ankles in a

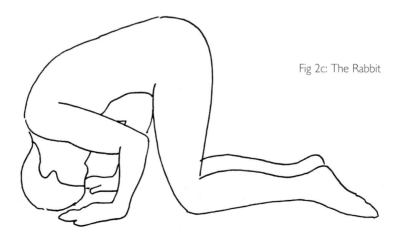

Fig 2c: The Rabbit

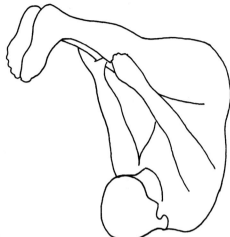

Fig 2d: The Pose of Tranquillity

comfortable position with no tension. Breathing normally, stay with the pose for ten seconds or only as long as it feels comfortable. To finish, roll your body slowly back to the floor.

THE PLOUGH
(Figure 2e)
This is a more difficult pose than the previous one, so you may like to work up to it gradually. It will release tension in the internal organs and promote flexibility in the shoulder and neck area, as well as regulate the pancreas and endocrine glands.

Follow the pose of tranquillity, but in this pose support your back with your hands, gently lowering your feet towards the floor. If you feel flexible and balanced enough, return your arms to the floor as illustrated. Breathing normally, hold the pose for ten seconds or for as long as you are comfortable. To finish, on an in-breath, slowly roll your body back to the floor.

Fig 2e: The Plough

20

THE GARUDASANA

(Figure 2f)

The garudasana consists of two stages: the first is the stretch of the eagle pose, and the second is the intertwining pose of the garudasana. The latter may initially take some practice, but your effort will be well rewarded with the inner balance which it brings.

Stand with your arms relaxed by your side, and take a few deep breaths. When you feel ready, on an in-breath, raise your arms, stretching them to reach for the sky in the pose of the eagle. Hold the pose for a few deep breaths. Breathing normally, fold your right leg around your left leg, and then your arms, with the left elbow on the top. Bend your left leg slightly to let your body bend forward into the twined eagle pose as illustrated. After a short time, slowly unwind yourself, and repeat the pose standing on the other leg, with the other arm on the top. Finding a point of focus at eye level helps balance, and standing against a wall is a good way initially to gain confidence.

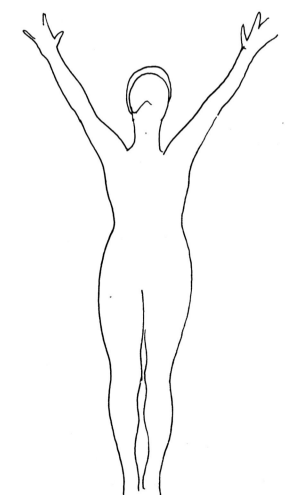

Fig 2f: The Garudasana

HEALING

Dr Carl Simonton, an oncologist, in his book 'Getting Well Again,' describes his pioneering work using orthodox and complementary medicine with cancer patients who were thought to be incurable. His patients are taught to meditate and visualize gaining control over their immune systems, and actively to remove cancerous cells from the body. Dr Simonton's work has been successful with many patients who had been thought to be terminally ill.

A NEW PERSPECTIVE

Quantum physics has brought a new perspective to the 'worldview' and the interconnectedness of ourselves and all living things in the universe. This draws us closer to an understanding of the Eastern mystical philosophies of Milarepa's worldview, in seeking to establish a relationship between the sense of self and consciousness.

Modern science and computer technologies have helped to bring a deeper understanding of the numerous powerful and empowering benefits which the practice of meditation has to its credit. Since earliest times meditation has been recognized as a spiritual endeavour, and one of the most effective ways of reaching the state of tranquillity and enlightenment.

We know also that the meditative state can also have important benefits for mental and physical health, and combined with visualization can bring about radical changes in both mind and body.

If the door of perception were cleansed
everything will appear to men as it is infinity.

(William Blake, 'The Marriage of Heaven and Hell')

The Auric Energy Field and Subtle Energies

*F*IGURE 3 SHOWS the multi-dimensional human being. The spine is the central axis surrounded by the five levels of subtle energy vibrations, all being part of our extended physical body.

The **etheric** level of vibration interfaces with the **physical** matter of the body; it underlies and energizes the physical, mental and spiritual aspects of being. As a receiver, it assimilates and transmits energies. Congestion of this level can be a major cause of illness.

The **astral** body is the domain of the emotions, eloquently described as 'a universal ocean of feeling', which allows us to unite with all beings. At this level, astral energies are received and transmitted via the throat chakra (see page 28) to the mental and physical body. As its purpose is primarily emotional expression, the emotional state of mind can be affected either in a positive way, promoting good health, or in a negative way, leading to disease.

Through their magnetic qualities, the astral and etheric bodies are able to attract other vibrations which resonate in harmony with them; for example, negative emotions attract others which 'adhere' themselves. Conversely, the etheric and astral bodies are equally capable of repelling emotions which are out of harmony, which can be realized when in close proximity to someone whose energy is felt to be uncomfortable.

The **mental** body is of a higher frequency than the etheric and astral. It is the medium for expression of the mind and intellect, of thoughts and ideas.

The **causal** body, the next level of subtle energy, is commonly believed to be the spiritual level and the medium of the higher self.

Research has shown that a connection and constant interplay exists between all things down to cellular level. Everything is energy, with nothing existing in isolation. Balance and harmony of all subtle energies is considered paramount to achieving and maintaining good health. These energies were invisible to all but gifted mystics and psychics who have been able to 'see' the different levels of the auric energy field, and to tune up to these levels with the purpose of balancing and harmonizing them in the process of healing.

KIRLIAN PHOTOGRAPHY

In the 1930s, these previously invisible auric vibrations were photographed in Russia by Semyon Kirlian, showing visible evidence to support the existence of an electrical energy field surrounding all living things. The aura around the body was seen to emanate in different colours and to alter in density according to health and

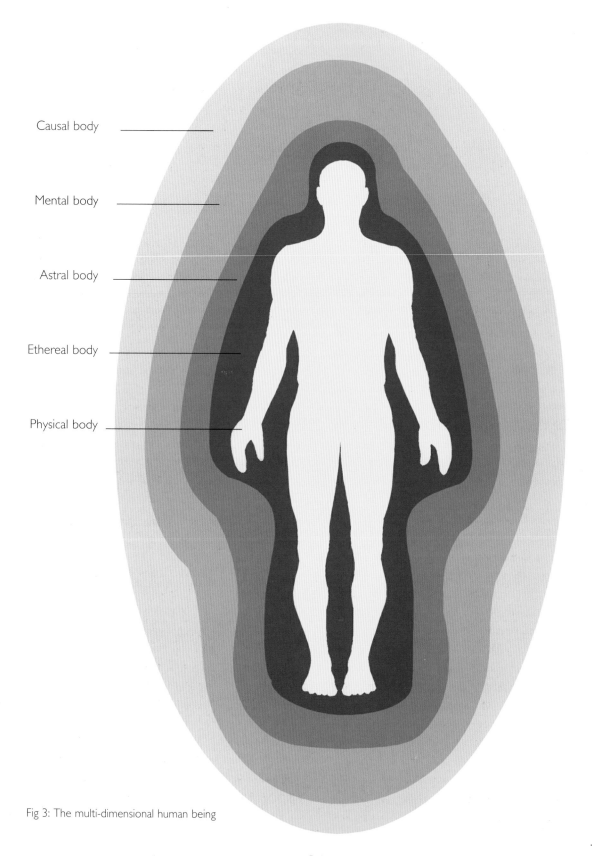

Causal body

Mental body

Astral body

Ethereal body

Physical body

Fig 3: The multi-dimensional human being

energy levels. Later, the rhythms of the mind were also monitored to reveal the vibrations of consciousness, showing the moods of the psyche.

Through research on his own energy field, Kirlian found that his state of health and level of vitality were markedly visible. When he felt his spirits to be down, his auric field was seen to be a dull and chaotic image; when his energy levels were high and he was in good spirits, there were beams of light radiating brightly.

Evidence that external electromagnetic fields can affect the body's natural field, both negatively and positively, was supplied by various experiments on the effect of energy through the body. Kirlian photographed an energy healer's hands in repose. As the healing on the patient progressed, subsequent photographs showed a massive increase in the emanations from the healer's hands, demonstrating our ability to alter our auric field by conscious thought, and also to affect other auric fields.

SUBTLE ENERGIES
IN HEALING

Vibrational or subtle energy healing was used and written about in Egypt as long as 2,500 years ago. The 'Ebers Papyrus', dated at around 1552 BC, talks of the laying-on of hands to heal illness. Seers of the ancient cultures had knowledge of how to benefit from the use of natural subtle energies. Yogis of Tibet and India utilized the power of the vibrations of the voice in overtone chanting, and chanting the OM sound to tone up their physical and mental condition. They did this by creating a balance and harmony in the energy field. The power of the voice was used by the shamans of the Navajo Indians to create pictures in sand. As we have seen, Kirlian photography has given us a visible picture of the electrical energy field surrounding all living things. Nikola Tesla, a twentieth-century physicist, stated: 'If the radiation of the cell can be returned to its original rhythm then it will resume its healthy state.'

The past few years have seen a growing acceptance of subtle energy principles in holistic healing. Energetic or vibrational healing, such as homeopathy, herbal medicine, spiritual healing and auric energy balancing, etc., have been redefined as complementary to orthodox medicine, rather than alternative. Computer technologies such as the MRI scan (magnetic resonance imager) image physical organs and help throw more light on the structure and workings of the body and brain.

Around 2,500 years ago, Pythagoras stated: 'All things are constructed on harmonic patterns.' Through science and computer technology we can now measure the characteristics of subtle energies to appreciate fully the importance of being in step with the natural harmonies of our being and in harmony with the energetic patterns of the universal rhythms.

BALANCING AND CENTRING
THE AURA

If you feel 'off-centre' or stressed, the following exercise is quick and effective.

EXERCISE

Sit in a chair facing a wall with no door or window openings. Cross your feet and arms, or place your hands on your knees, to create a closed circuit. Visualize a scene or an image to occupy your mind; at the same time, feel your energy flowing round your body in a circle. Continue for as long as you hold the image. Relax. Give thanks.

Chakras

CHAKRAS WERE WRITTEN about in the ancient scriptures of the east. The word chakra is derived from Sanskrit, and means 'a wheel'. Chakras have been recognized as energy vortices or power points through which energies spiral into our aura and subtle auric energy field.

Dr Carl Jung equates the chakras as being 'the gateways of consciousness in man, receptive points for the inflow of energies from the cosmos and the spirit and soul of man'. As we saw in the previous chapter, these energies emanating from the body can be photographed, and they can also be seen by some gifted mystics and healers.

The chakras lie down the spine and correspond to the plexuses, a network of nerves, blood vessels and fibres in the physical body. Each chakra is associated with a major nerve plexus and a major endocrine gland. In the holistic principle of spiritual healing, yoga and so on, the chakras are perceived as a natural law and their balance as central to vitality and good health.

The prime function of the chakras is to receive, assimilate and distribute the subtle energies throughout the body. The energies can be cosmic rays or originate from the collective unconscious of the earth. Balance of this process is fundamental to the body being in perfect harmony with emotions, mind and spirit, with the energy centres connecting to the multi-dimensional universe.

Our ability to access higher energetic information relies on the proper alignment and working of the chakras and subtle bodies of energy. When the energy in the chakras is low or out of alignment through anxiety, fear or illness the body's energies are in a contracted state.

The chakras can become damaged and blocked by physical accident, emotional shock or fear. These experiences can upset the balance of the endocrine system, with the possibility of psychological disorder. Research has shown that the 'self' becomes 'whole' when all the chakras representing all the aspects of being are balanced and focused in harmony. Alice Bailey, in her book *Esoteric Healing*, states: 'The new medical science will be outstandingly built upon the science of the centres, and upon this knowledge all diagnosis and possible cure will be based.'

THE SEVEN CHAKRAS

The **base chakra** (also known as the root chakra) has its physical counterpart as the adrenal glands and governs the area of the spinal column and the kidneys. It supports all the other chakras. It is described in ancient Indian wisdom as a channel for the will to be, linking us to the life force of nature, and is the seat of the kundalini force (see page 28). The corresponding colour of the base chakra is red. It controls vitality and confidence and our connection to the earth.

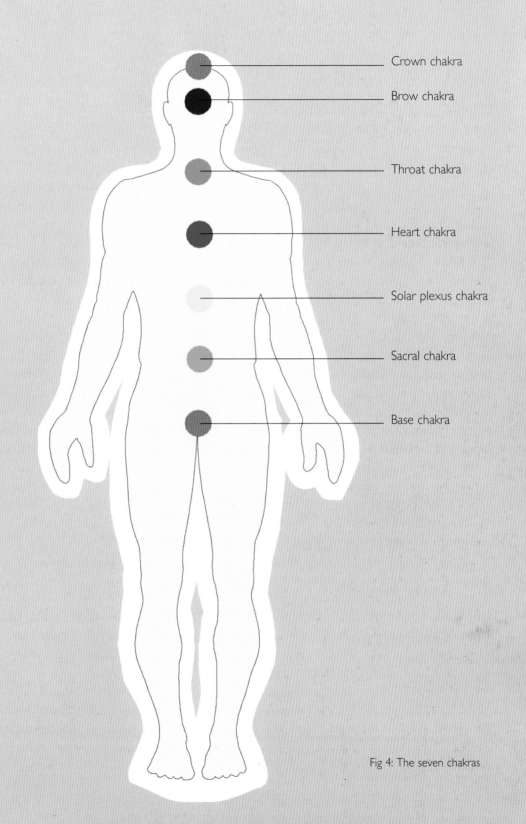

Crown chakra

Brow chakra

Throat chakra

Heart chakra

Solar plexus chakra

Sacral chakra

Base chakra

Fig 4: The seven chakras

The **sacral chakra** (or splenic chakra), positioned at the midpoint below the navel, has its counterpart in the gonads, the ovaries or testicles, which produce hormones for sexual development and the reproductive cycle. The hormones have an effect on the entire personality. The energy, in addition to being sexual, can be channelled into more conscious levels of creativity: art, music, writing etc. Orange is the colour of the sacral chakra and controls sexuality and sensual emotion.

The **solar plexus chakra** has its counterpart in the pancreas, governing the stomach, liver, gall bladder and nervous and digestive systems. The solar plexus is often the place where energy blockages occur. Its colour is yellow, which radiates joyousness and optimism. It is the centre of our instinctive feeling, controlling personal power and how we view ourselves in relation to others and life in general.

The **heart chakra** has its counterpart in the thymus gland, which is important in the regulation of the immune response. The flow of subtle energies through the heart chakra rebalances and aligns the energies of all the chakras. It is through the heart chakra that we express love towards the self, and love towards others. It is represented by the colour green, the colour of nature and balance. Total balance of this chakra brings experience of unconditional love, and an increase of soul energy.

The **throat chakra** has its counterpart in the thyroid gland, influencing the way we express ourselves and communicate with others. Blockages and imbalances in this centre can be caused by difficulties with self-expression, the inability to communicate true inner feelings or recognize personal needs. It is represented by the colour blue, a peaceful colour that moves away from the physical towards the spiritual aspects of life, uplifting the mind.

The **brow chakra** is located behind the centre of the forehead, and its physical counterpart is the pituitary gland, also being associated with the third eye and psychic abilities. This chakra governs intuition, clairvoyance and awareness. Meditation helps to develop this centre by opening it to receiving energies from the higher realms of spirit. Clairvoyance means clear vision, and difficulties in the area of the brow chakra, such as sinus, eye, nose and ear, could originate in a reluctance to acknowledge important messages for the soul's progress. It is represented by the colour indigo with its ability to calm fears and inhibitions, and to bring understanding and clarity to the nature of physical and spiritual aspects of being.

The **crown chakra** is located at the top of the head, it has its physical counterpart in the pineal gland, influencing spiritual progress. The crown chakra is considered to be the highest vibrational centre in the subtle energy body. The opening of the crown chakra coincides with the balance and alignment of all the chakras. This is our entry to the highest state of consciousness. The colour for the crown chakra is violet, which through meditation and contemplation offers insight into the meaning of life.

KUNDALINI

Kundalini is a Sanskrit word meaning 'circular power'. It is associated with the base chakra, which supports all the other chakras, being the link to the life force of nature. The base chakra is regarded as the seat of the energy of the kundalini. In the many references in ancient Eastern literature, the kundalini is represented as a coiled serpent with male and female polarities, which spiral up around the spine, lifting consciousness into higher spiritual levels. The coiled serpent is symbolic of a powerful energy poised to spring into action.

The powerful subtle energies of the kundalini usually raise naturally during meditation, when all the chakras are open and in alignment, and the energy flow unimpeded. This is dependent upon the individual's level of emotion and spiritual attainment.

There are known methods of arousing the kundalini forces, although the author agrees with the many people who view this practice as potentially dangerous, even under the guidance of a teacher. Many nervous breakdowns and mid-life crises are in fact spiritual transformations, triggered by the awakening of the kundalini force, which occasionally can be dramatic; these have been aptly named a 'spiritual emergency' by Christina and Stanislav Grof in their invaluable book *The Stormy Search For The Self*.

Seven-Colour Spectrum Visualization Aid

*T*HE IMPORTANCE OF colour vibrations and their effect on our body and soul has been outlined on page 13. We witness the seven colour rays naturally when they manifest as a rainbow, which is the result of refraction and internal reflection of light in raindrops. Instinctively we know that the translucent colours are of a higher vibration, and the soul registers pleasure at their sighting.

The colours which we need collectively as a community or nation manifest in the colours of seasonal foods, or in fashion as a fashion statement of cosmic consciousness; they are the colours we need at the time as part of our evolution to help us attune to the higher vibrations which are now coming to the planet.

This visualization aid can be used with any of the exercises or meditations: take a few seconds to look at the colour which you are meditating on. When you close your eyes try to recreate it in your mind's eye – visualizing the colours will come naturally in time.

Meditating on the colour spectrum can also revitalize the energies in the body, and lift the spirits, and can also be used as a breathing exercise to assist healing. (This exercise can be practised effectively by visualizing the colours without looking at the colour rays, but when using it the vibrations of the colours are absorbed naturally into the system.)

EXERCISE

Take a few deep breaths. When you are relaxed, breathe in the colours, letting them gently permeate your entire being. Direct them to places of discomfort or illness within the mind and body, visualizing them dissolving energy blockages and sweeping them away in the clear flow of energy.

A COLOUR MEDITATION FOR CLEARING AND BALANCING THE CHAKRAS

This is a wonderfully relaxing meditation. In addition to clearing and balancing the chakras, it is a good exercise for centring thought. It can transport the mind, body and spirit, lifting them above the day-to-day mundane. Allow approximately 40 minutes for this meditation. After a while you may want to extend it beyond that time, but go at your own pace, finding your own comfort level. It looks long, but it is easy to memorize. Let the energy flow in a circular motion, whichever way feels comfortable.

time to enjoy a connection with your spirit guides, and experience the reciprocal energy of love.

Raise your awareness to the brow chakra, behind the centre of the forehead. Let the vibrant white light spin in the centre, clearing and balancing the brow chakra. As the white light expands, it slowly changes into indigo light, a rich clear deep blue. Feel the psychic centres opening as clear channels of intuition, integration, knowing and inspiration. Take time to link into the realms of pure consciousness.

Now, lift your awareness to the crown chakra, on the top of your head. Let the white light spin in the centre, clearing and balancing the crown chakra. As it expands, it slowly changes to pure clear violet light. Let the violet light flow gently through your mind, body, spirit and aura. Know that your focus and balance will be invaluable to yourself, and others. Take time to experience the love that permeates the realms of the highest vibration. Give thanks.

When you are ready, and in your own time, slowly count back from ten to one, grounding yourself in the present. Take a few deep breaths, stretch your body, and open your eyes. Give thanks.

When you have established your own timing and rhythm for the meditation you may find it helpful to record your own tape. The meditation is suitable, and enjoyable, to do with a group, taking it in turns to direct the meditation.

ARM CIRCLING COLOUR MEDITATION FOR REVITALIZING ENERGIES AND CHAKRA BALANCING

This exercise has a wonderfully revitalizing effect and takes ten minutes or so. It involves circling the arms and at the same time visualizing each of the seven colour rays of the chakras in turn. If you find it helpful, use the colour visualization aid on page 31.

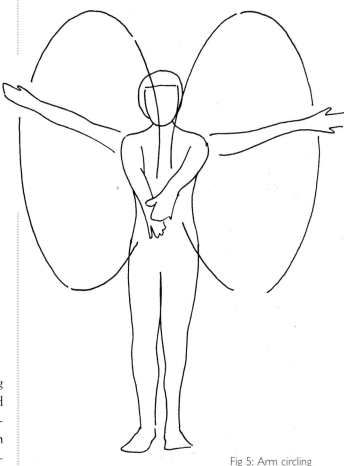

Fig 5: Arm circling colour meditation

EXERCISE

Stand with feet comfortably apart, hands and arms relaxed by your sides. Take a few deep breaths. Joining your index finger and thumb, visualize holding a vibrant red colour of the base chakra between them. Swing your arms forward and over your head in a circle, visualizing your hands tracing a circle of red light. When your hands are at your sides again, change and join your thumb with the second finger, visualizing a clear orange of the sacral chakra. Swing your arms forward and over your head, visualizing a circle of orange light. Continue through all the seven colours and chakras, progressing through to join all the fingers in turn.

I DREAMT

I dreamt that the world was a kinder place, with all beings enjoying the space.

I dreamt that the world acknowledged human endeavour, including of those not gifted and clever.

I dreamt that the world was less judgemental, looking instead for human potential.

I dreamt that the world promoted creativity, with beauty and love overpowering negativity.

I dreamt that the world knew that, by its thoughts, it would create the environment it sought.

I dreamt that the world had used its intent, greed and darkness finally forced to relent.

I dreamt that the world had woken up, taking it upon itself to re-write the book.

Left and Right Brain Balancing

ANCIENT CULTURE RECOGNIZED that balance between the right and left brain hemispheres was vital to mental health, and also for perceiving the universe from a holistic viewpoint. The left and right sides of the brain are two different, yet complementary, aspects of consciousness, with both sides contributing specialized capabilities.

The left brain represents our analytical thought, dealing with mathematics, reading, writing and the rational world of daily experience. It controls the contractions of muscles on the right side of the body, the right eye and the right ear. The right brain deals with images and emotions, expressing our artistic, abstract, intuitive and spiritual aspects. It controls the left side of the body, the left ear and the left eye. Meditation, art, music, dreaming and most creative activities connect us to the right hemisphere of the brain. Balance of our two brain hemispheres allows for expression of full expanded consciousness. Many complicated activities, such as reading and writing, rely on using both hemispheres simultaneously working together.

Modern computer science is able to monitor the brain's activity using the CAP (computerized automatic psychophysiological) scan which registers the brain's action as colour images on a screen, confirming that dominance is constantly shifting from right to left and from left to right and that we need to develop both sides to become well-balanced people.

The electrical activity of the brain can be measured by an electroencephalogram (EEG). Study has shown that certain brainwaves correspond to particular mental states. Alpha waves occur at frequencies of 8-13 cycles per second. During this state there is a decrease in oxygen consumption, blood pressure and the heart rate drops. This level is characteristic of meditation, deep relaxation and hypnosis. Beta waves have frequencies of 14-50 cycles per second and we experience them in the hypnogogic state, just before falling asleep and just before waking; most dreams occur at this level. Delta waves are below 3-5 cycles per second, which we experience in deep sleep.

In the past century, the qualities of left-brain rational thinking were highly valued and needed in the rational mechanistic era, while the right brain's artistic, intuitive and psychic qualities of expression fell into neglect somewhat, and were thought to be unreliable and suspect.

The two hemispheres are said to have differing time modes. Physicist Robert Oppenheimer, in referring to the two sides of the brain, wrote: 'These two ways of thinking, the way of time and history and the way of eternity and timelessness, are both part of man's effort to comprehend the world in which he lives. Neither is comprehended in the other, nor reducible to it . . . each supplementing the other – neither telling the whole story.'

Below are two exercises for the balance of the brain, the figure-of-eight and the labyrinth.

THE FIGURE-OF-EIGHT EXERCISE

This represents a cross-pattern exercise to promote the co-operation and balance of the two hemispheres of the brain (see Figure 6).

EXERCISE

Starting with the index finger on the left hand, trace the figure-of-eight three times following the arrows. Change hands to repeat with the right hand. Repeat the sequence three times.

The figure-of-eight exercise can also be used in the following way. Stand upright with arms extended out in front and parallel to the ground, hands held together with palms flat. Keeping the arms straight, trace the figure-of-eight in the air in front of you.

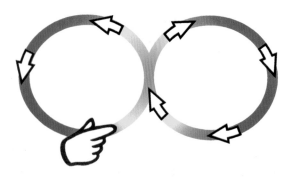

Fig 6: The figure-of eight exercise

THE LABYRINTH EXERCISE

Figure 7 shows the classical seven-coil labyrinth, which often goes by the name of 'Troy'. Although they are to be found throughout the ancient world, the only turf version to be found in Britain is in Terrington, Yorkshire. This classical labyrinth design is also to be seen on old Cretan coins, and carved on walls across the world. Labyrinths take the walker on a journey to the centre, unlike the design of a maze, in which the walker can get lost. For the purpose of this book, the centre of the labyrinth represents the centre of the brain, and like the previous exercise is also a cross-pattern.

Fig 7: The seven-coil labyrinth

EXERCISE

Using the blunt end of a pen or pencil in the right hand as a pointer, enter the labyrinth and make the journey to the centre. Then, returning to the entrance, change to the left hand, repeat the journey to the centre and back. Repeat this sequence once or twice more.

Preparing For Meditation

*Y*OUR SACRED MEDITATION space can be designed to be a retreat from the mundane world, a place which helps you link to your higher self and the higher realms of consciousness, a space to expand your conscious mind to explore the cosmos, or a haven to relax in. It can be a refuge, offering a retreat to revive your energies, renew your spirit and soothe your soul.

Choosing a quiet area where you will be undisturbed is ideal. Be it a small corner or an entire room, it makes no difference if you create it to reflect your own individuality. Use colours and textures that please you, and that have good associations for you. Working to a sense of harmony with your environment means that you will find it relaxing and nurturing.

Set aside a table or area to accommodate candles, incense, plants, crystals, inspirational pictures, statues and other items that you enjoy having around you. Music also can be wonderfully relaxing and inspirational. The healing and calming powers of music and rhythm have been recognized since early times. We have an amazing selection to choose from, but check that it resonates comfortably with you during meditation, whatever your choice.

The music of Bach, Beethoven, Mozart and Handel is said to be inspired by the cosmic music of the spheres. Many people prefer ambient music, Indian Ayurvedic vibrational tapes or sounds of dolphins for meditation. You may like to record your own personal tapes: the sound of ocean waves, for example, or the sounds of the forest – birds and wind in the trees. Listening to your own recording helps to recapture the environment quickly and enjoy it with all your senses – a communion with nature.

Try to ensure that the area is warm enough and draught-free. A cosy rug is good to have to hand. Whichever way you choose to sit, make sure that you are comfortable and centred, with your spine in its natural position. If you are not comfortable sitting on the floor, meditation seats may be a good idea; they are used by many experienced meditators. Spaces that we use frequently resonate with our vibrations. You may wish to make an affirmation before entering your sacred space, such as: 'As I enter my sacred space, I resolve to purify my thoughts, leaving behind my daily concerns. I raise my vibrations to link with the higher realms of the cosmos.'

Always remember to clear the energies regularly, and immediately after a group meditation. You will find the exercise for space clearing below.

CLEARING AND CREATING A PURE SPACE

The atmosphere or 'vibes' in a room or building are often high on the list of our memories of that place. We can immediately sense through the vibrations whether it is welcoming and comfortable, or uneasy and threatening.

The power of words spoken with bitterness and anger in a room can linger on, destroying the tranquillity for a very long time. The energy of the voice is a powerful way of transmitting both good and bad vibrations. At best it can convey the most beautiful sentiments, calm, reassure and heal. Conversely, negative thoughts and words upset the equilibrium of mind and body, and disturb the balance and harmony in a room.

A small container of salt placed by the phone will absorb any negative energies from telephone conversations. (Remember to change the salt frequently, and wash all crystals regularly, letting water run over them, as they retain all the absorbed energies.) If you anticipate receiving a non-urgent call, with a potential for causing anger and negativity, consider giving things time to settle down. Put the answerphone on, or be busy elsewhere for a while. Many words spoken in the heat of the moment are not meant, but the energies in your room and your energy field have no way of knowing that. Taoism advises that it is better to lie low when the wind blows hard than to strive against the storm.

Feng Shui suggests many ways to clear spaces: music, singing, chanting, candles, burning sage or sandalwood and sprinkling salt water over the area are all effective ways to clear and purify space. The following exercise clears and purifies any area and is a powerful way of revitalizing the energies. Stand in the middle of the space.

EXERCISE

Take a few minutes to breathe deeply and relax. Request help and protection from the spirits of light and spirit guides. As you breathe rhythmically, on the outbreath let your energy expand into a purifying white light, slowly filling the entire room. As it flows into all the corners, affirm that you are clearing, cleansing and revitalizing all the energy. Request protection for the whole house. Give thanks.

CLEARING THE BODY AND AURA

Anyone who has had the misfortune to live or work in an environment laden with negative energies will know just how destructive it can become to the essential quality of life. The following exercise to clear your body and aura can be used in any situation and practised quickly if need be. It is equally effective sitting, standing or lying down.

EXERCISE

Take a few deep breaths, and allow yourself to relax. State your intent to purify your body and aura. Visualize or sense a vibrant violet flame flowing strongly from the centre of the earth. Let it flow upwards through your body and aura, cleansing and purifying every cell, and carrying away any negative energies. Watch the flame reach a point high above your head, then turn and cascade downwards, returning to the centre of the earth, where it will transmute, back into the pure energy of nature. Give thanks.

One of the most ancient remedies for neutralizing negativity is the use of crystalline salt, which has been highly valued by many cultures throughout history. A simple and effective way of clearing and purifying the body and the aura is to soak in a salt bath (one pound of Epsom salts, dissolved in plenty of hot water). It can be a really enjoyable and relaxing experience. Allow plenty of time, perhaps lighting candles, burning incense and playing music. As you relax in the water, visualize or sense that the salt is absorbing any negativity and your energy is being grounded in the centre of the earth. The salt bath is a perfect place to meditate, or just to be.

Another quick way to clear your energies is to let the water in the shower cascade over your body, affirming that any negative energies are being washed away in the flow of water. For those lucky enough to be able to swim in the sea, that is the ideal.

Dreams

OST CULTURES OF the ancient world have placed a high value on the interpretation of dreams, and have taken them very seriously. One of the earliest records is the dream book of Artemidorus of Ephesus in the second century AD. There were also Greek sleep temples and a Dream God Oneiros. Healers of that time used the art of oneiromany as a means of divination by dreams to foretell the prognosis of an illness, and to find a cure.

Dreams are a form of symbolic communication; the higher self can use dreams to transmit information from the soul to the conscious mind, and they act as an outlet for releasing tension from the mind and body. Through dreams we are able to transcend the mundane world and link with the higher realms of consciousness. This is the domain of the right brain, that of intuition and spiritual activity which interacts closer to the higher self. Wakefulness is the domain of the left brain, although in the wakeful state we need to use both hemispheres of the brain.

Most of our dreams occur in the Alpha state (see page 000), just before falling asleep and just before being fully awake. Research has shown that dreams are essential for physical and mental health. Experiments to deprive individuals deliberately of their dreams resulted in hallucinations and mental disturbance after a short period of time in some individuals.

Mystics and shamans have recognized the potential of manipulating dreams, using them to enhance psychic powers and promote greater creativity, and using them as channels through which they are able to transcend the physical world to commune with the higher realms.

DREAM JOURNAL

Documenting and learning to interpret our dreams is a creative activity, presenting an opportunity for deeper self-understanding, and awakening intuitive abilities.

In the waking state, dreams tend to vanish quickly from the memory, so document your dreams in your dream journal as soon as possible; if you can only recall fragments, jot them down, and with practice you will remember more and more. When you read the journal later, try to analyse the origin: are they a means of releasing tension from the mind and body, messages from the soul, or guidance and wisdom from the higher realms of intelligence? Are they probable solutions to problems, or long-buried emotions surfacing for you to resolve and transcend?

After a time, you may notice a pattern emerging, which can also be helpful in the process of learning to analyse your dreams and become aware of the extraordinary creativity, innovation and power of the brain, and the liberating qualities of dreams.

INTERPRETING AND USING DREAMS

Important messages often appear to pre-empt situations which could become problematical. Chris had set up home in an idyllic setting; she had created a space in which to work and be creative, and enjoy life. It was rural but a long journey from her friends and colleagues.

In her dream, she was working in the cellar of a house which she knew was her home. The doorbell rang and, as she tried to answer it, the cellar door jammed and she missed the caller. She continued working and some time later the bell rang again, and the same thing happened; the caller was unable to contact her. Chris knew in the dream that she was being shown how cut-off and inaccessible she had become.

Although maybe we are unaware of it, natural healing takes place in the dream state. Jane Roberts in *The Nature of Personal Reality* writes: 'Nightmares in series are often inner-regulated shock therapy. They may frighten the conscious self considerably, but after all it comes awake in its normal world, shaken but secure in the framework of the day.' (From the book *The Nature of Personal Reality* © 1994, Jane Roberts. Reprinted by permission of Amber-Allen Publishing Inc., PO Box 6657, San Rafael, CA 94903. All rights reserved.)

There are many cases of lives saved by people acting upon their dreams, changing plans and avoiding tragedy. As we have seen (page 54), scientists, artists and writers have all received inspiration through dreams; for example, Niels Bohr had help with the structure of the atom, and it won him the Nobel Prize.

Potential

ONE OF THE MAIN requirements for attaining enlightenment is thought by many people to be the development of personal potential. Left to its own devices, our higher self will guide us through our lives, happily negotiating sequences of events that will lead us to a realization of potential and spiritual awareness. The information-technology era has supplied us with a constant flow of information and knowledge; the down side, however, is that our mind's databank, which also receives important internal information, can reach overload, resulting in vital messages for our welfare and creative processes going unheeded. How often have you had recurring ideas for a creative project, or had a vision of how you could fulfil your desire for a change in lifestyle, and not acted upon them?

The higher self, mainly through intuition, constantly tries to initiate the next step along 'the way' it also sends messages through dreams, sometimes trauma or simply knowing. Contemplation, meditation and involvement in creative activities all offer opportunities to be silent, and to listen for guidance and inspiration from the higher self and the higher realms of consciousness.

BELIEFS

How we perceive ourselves – our talents and abilities – in relationship to others and the universe helps to form our beliefs. Unexamined beliefs and information become our reality. This applies equally to positive and negative false beliefs and can be just as self-limiting.

Clare sought hypnotherapy to help understand why she had always been non-assertive in her life; she felt that she was not reaching her potential. During the hypnotherapy session, Clare regressed to her early childhood. Her large family had only sufficient seating around the table for the family members. When a visitor joined them for a meal, Clare's mother always told Clare to give up her seat and sit at a little side table to make room for the visitor. This was always met with great approval from her mother. One of Clare's early beliefs was that stepping aside to make room for others is a very good way to be, and so it is, within reason.

Imagine for a moment that the world's governments had imposed a ban on anyone whose paintings could not match the talent of the Old Masters, anyone playing sport below Olympic Games standard or writing music not equal to Mozart, Beethoven, Bach, and so on. Would you find the concept ridiculous, not to mention a gross infringement of human rights? Yet many people voluntarily impose such bans on themselves, constantly reinforcing them with obsolete, false or negative beliefs.

Misconceptions and misunderstandings in relation to our personal reality interfere with clear vision, clouding and distorting perception. They convert the personal quest for enlightenment and fulfilment into an obstacle course and delay progress.

SERIOUS SOUL-SEARCHING

Are you following your own dreams and visions, or tailoring yourself to gain approval, and to be compatible with someone else's ideals? Are you exploring your own inner dreams, desires and ambitions, and seeking out all the opportunities to bring them into being? Do you nurture false beliefs about your worthiness to be happy and successful? Goethe, the German philosopher, wrote: 'Whatever you think you can do or believe you can do begin it now. Action has magic, grace and power in it.'

The following example looks at the same thing, but in a new way. Marie had been accepted to work as a volunteer in a hospital for severely mentally and physically challenged children. On her first day, as she waited for the head doctor to arrive, Marie desperately wondered what sort of contribution she would be able to make. When the doctor arrived, he explained that the ethos of the department was to encourage the children to reach their potential, for example if a child managed to feed him/herself one spoonful of food in the day then that should be celebrated as a success. Marie's perception of her role and the contribution which it was possible for her to make was changed by this positive ethos, and she went on to fulfil her desire to make a substantial contribution to the department.

If you see what is small as it sees itself, and accept what is weak for what strength it has, and use what is dim for the light it gives then all is well. This is called Acting Naturally.

(Lao-Tsu, Tao Teh King)

Crisis

THE MEDIEVAL MYSTIC Meister Eckhart wrote: 'Truly, it is in the darkness that one finds the light. So when we are in sorrow, then this light is nearest to all of us.' You may have been surprised, in looking back to a previous situation, at the amazing supply of energy and inner resources which helped you to pull through. So it will be with any crisis that you are working through in this moment. In the blueprint of our journey in this life, only structures that are within our power to transcend will be presented to us by the soul.

Every crisis has its own agenda, and can be met as an opportunity to take another step along the path of enlightenment, offering potential for moving forward into a deeper understanding of ourselves. An honest appraisal of the crisis will often reveal changes needed in perception, beliefs and lifestyle, to restore balance and harmony in the ecology of mind, body, spirit and emotions. Ask your higher self: 'What am I to learn from this? What is the message?' The solution may come in dream form, or clarity will reveal a possible solution.

Elisabeth Kubler-Ross offers this invaluable advice: 'Learn to get in touch with the silence within yourself and know that every single thing in this life has a purpose.' Trusting in life's purpose, and our own destiny within the greater plan – even though in times of crisis it can be obscure to the point of seemingly non-existent – does restore inner peace and eases feelings of isolation and alienation.

Daily meditation keeps the channels open to the higher self and the spirit realms to receive information and clarity of mind. Ask for guidance and an understanding of the issues that you are working with. Often a solution can be found to complex problems after the main issues have been identified and viewed as a priority. Goethe wrote: 'Things which matter most should never be at the mercy of things which matter least.'

In choosing to talk to a trusted friend, ensure that focus is kept on the real issues involved. Any decisions that you make must be true to your own integrity if they are to be effective in the long term. After all, it is your personal journey.

Seth, a spirit quoted by Jane Roberts in *The Nature of Personal Reality*, has these words of encouragement: 'When you ask for advice and direction in your life, to some extent you keep from yourself the realization that you yourself possess it.' (From the book *The Nature of Personal Reality* © 1994, Jane Roberts. Reprinted by permission of Amber-Allen Publishing Inc., PO Box 6657, San Rafael, CA 94903. All rights reserved.)

WHAT TO DO IN A CRISIS

- Keep yourself warm.

- Take some deep breaths.

- Seek help. This is very important.

- Speak to a friend or someone who can give

comfort and encouragement until the crisis subsides.

- If no-one is available, look in the telephone book under CRISIS or ask Enquiries for the contact number.

- When you feel calmer, find a therapist, such as a spiritual or psychic healer, energy balancer or body worker, crisis counsellor etc (not all of them charge a fee).

- Respond to the crisis from your own true nature; people in crisis sometimes act out of character and compound their problems.

- Ask for help from your higher self and spirit guides.

- Have courage to have faith and believe in yourself.

- When you are able to understand the nature of the crisis, and what is causing it, you are well on the way to overcoming it.

The following exercises will help you calm and empower yourself in crisis, as well as restore balance and comfort.

EXERCISE

Raise both arms as high as you can above your head. Grasp energy with both hands, bringing your arms down slowly, bending the elbows as you bring them down. Visualize yourself pulling powerful energy into your body. Repeat the exercise several times. (This is also an exercise of intent, empowering you, as you are taking positive steps to overcome the crisis.)

EXERCISE

Sit upright in a chair, with feet flat on the floor. Wrap your arms around your body in a hug. Rock back and forward gently in a rhythmical motion. After a few minutes, try to synchronize your breathing with the rocking. Continue until you feel a sense of calmness returning. Finish with the previous exercise of pulling energy into your system to empower yourself.

PHYSICAL AND MENTAL ILLNESS

Many illnesses and addictions are the result of losing touch with our natural rhythms and those of the universe. Symptoms are messages telling us that we are not living our truth. Many crises occur when buried emotions and experiences rise to the surface and need to be worked through and released. They can arise when the individual starts to explore their ways of being, as opposed to their achievements by ways of doing. Single-minded pursuits of a set goal, to the exclusion of all else, and lack of creative and spiritual expression, can throw the system into imbalance.

SPIRITUAL DEVELOPMENT CRISIS

The transformational journey of spiritual development is a move toward wholeness. This evolutionary process has been recognized by almost every culture throughout the ages, with ceremonies and initiations marking the various stages. For many people this is a gradual, natural process of gaining insight through experience and working towards personal potential. For others it can be dramatic and devastating to their life. In their excellent book, *The Stormy Search For The Self*, Christina and Stanislav Grof have presented a deeper understanding of the profound personal transformation of spiritual opening and the possible challenges that it presents.

Understanding, support and encouragement are of the essence in spiritual crisis management. Search to find people who have a deep understanding of the situation. Do not go it alone. Spiritual healers and many complementary therapists and doctors will be able to help or suggest appropriate avenues for you to explore.

Looking back on their experiences in crisis, many people claim it as a liberating process, a healing of the spirit and soul, with radical shifts in their perception of themselves and their values. Danish author and mystic Soren Kierkegaard held an energetic view of crisis. He proclaimed: 'You are in utter despair about yourself? Good. That is a needed step towards liberation. But you must face your despair fully and deeply and not lull yourself to sleep with comforting doctrines or shallow escape. Face the fact of being what you are, for that is what

changes what you are. Far from being your shame and ruin, honest self-observation leads to the very salvation for which you would gladly give everything.' Many post-crisis individuals would confirm the validity of these words.

For example, Diana's crisis was the catalyst for a new, rich and rewarding life. Over a number of years, the stress of Diana's work had resulted in a nervous breakdown. As part of her recovery programme, she joined an occupational therapy group. Offered a choice of arts and crafts, Diana chose painting, which she had always dreamt of doing one day but had never found the time. Not only did the painting restore balance and harmony in her being, but Diana also developed her talent to use later in a successful commercial venture.

Do not think of disillusionment as a sad thing, we think this state is terrible — we are mistaken. It is there that we find peace and liberty.

(François Fenelon)

Letting Go of the Past

LIVING IN THE PRESENT

Yesterday is a cancelled cheque
Tomorrow is a promissory note
Today is cash in hand, spend it Wisely
(Anon)

It has been said that when we say we have 'unfinished business' what we really mean is that we did not like the way things ended. It does seem to be part of the human condition, though, that most of us have had some past experiences that we need to release, acknowledge and then let go of, at some point on the spiritual journey.

The past is our personal history, where we can learn about ourselves, our relationship with others and how we fit into the universe. How successful we are in moving forward into a fulfilling and creative future rests largely on how we choose to view our past, and process it. If we are able to recognize and develop the positive, good things, and to transcend the negative aspects, it then becomes possible to express our true individuality.

A client in a hypnotherapy session saw the negative events in her past as two heavy bags, which had been weighing her down for quite a few years. Another felt that he had a heavy weight resting on his shoulders. The negative memories that are carried through life sap energy, with the true, unencumbered, light self always having a struggle to surface.

Negative emotions, such as anger and depression, are often carried forward into the present. Many are of unknown origin, the cause long forgotten or buried in the cellular memory. These negative emotions can become part of our reality, colouring our perceptions and adversely affecting the decisions that we make.

Holding on to the past blocks the natural flow of energy through the physical body, eventually causing disease. Good health relies on inner calm and balance. Have you noticed how negative thoughts and energies can inhibit spontaneity of life, robbing us of our joy and vitality?

Often the past surfaces at an appropriate time, especially when we are ready to take another step forward on the journey towards awareness. The process of letting go can present a wonderful opportunity to make a quantum leap into a more fulfilling future.

When you feel ready and comfortable to let go of your past, try the affirmation for letting go, given below. As you repeat this affirmation for four or five consecutive days, you will become aware that it is addressing issues of personal power and taking charge of your life.

THE AFFIRMATION FOR LETTING GO

My intention is to forgive everyone in my past, and to thank them for the wisdom and the knowledge that I now have. I cannot know the full purpose and implication of all the experiences at this time, but I place my trust in the greater plan for this planet and my role within it.

I am letting go of the past now; releasing negativity from my cellular memory and moving forward, taking only the positive knowledge, wisdom and experience, which I will use for the highest good of all concerned, my new way of being.

I am now free and detached from old negative thought patterns, and able to view the past with unconditional love.

SACRED RITE FOR RELEASING ANGER AND HURT

Releasing emotions through the written word is a very therapeutic method of clearing mind, body and spirit.

Write a letter to the individual or parties involved (for your eyes only). Fully express your innermost feelings, explaining why you are hurt, angry and distraught, and so on. Write only your true feelings, not seeking revenge. When you have finished, set up your sacred rite, burning the letter in a dish or open fire. As the letter burns, visualize your mind and body being purified by the release of these emotions, stating your desire to move forward in your life. Give thanks.

Good Health and Self-Healing

ARILYN FERGUSON, in her book *The Aquarian Conspiracy*, states: 'The healer inside us is the wisest, most complex integrated entity in the Universe.' This innate potential ability to heal ourselves is one of our most precious gifts.

In the development of a holistic sense of self, we arrive at a deeper understanding of the interrelatedness of physical, mental, emotional and energetic levels of our being. The holistic approach treats these aspects as complementary and inseparable from each other.

Conscious beliefs about ourselves and the nature of illness play a vital role in assisting or hindering our abilities to maintain good health. Expectations that illness goes hand in hand with the territory of life, and especially in advanced years, programmes the 'body intelligence' with false and negative signals, almost amounting to giving yourself permission to be ill. Negative beliefs can be reversed at any time by simply 'a change of mind' and re-shaping thoughts, making an affirmation to take control of our own health.

During illness there are imbalances in the flow of energies throughout the system. An example of the effect of changing the energy balances by a positive outlook is the case of a patient who was so ill that his doctor believed he had only three months to live. The patient chose to try to enjoy his remaining time by staying in bed and watching the funniest comedy films he could find. Over a period of time his condition gradually improved. Laughter was the tonic which brought about biochemical changes in his system, and he progressed on to enjoy his recovery.

Three of the most effective tonics for health are enthusiasm, optimism and humour. All three of these wonderful attributes can be developed by anyone, free of charge, requiring only as much effort as it takes to change one's mind into positive mode. Positive thoughts are also contagious, so not only do you make important positive changes to your own life but you also change the atmosphere for the benefit of those around you.

STRESS

One of the most common causes of stress is constant overload on the mental and physical systems. General symptoms include lack of concentration, insomnia, exhaustion, depression, anxiety, lack of inner peace and serenity. Symptoms are messages from the wisdom of the inner self, urging us to assess our lifestyle and thought patterns. The first thing to do is establish the issues involved, that is what is causing your stress. Sit in a meditative state and visualize yourself going through your past week. The following list will help check possible causes:

- Adequate quality of sleep
- Nourishing diet – eating in a relaxed way
- Vitamins, minerals and trace elements
- Fresh air and exercise
- Balance of work and relaxation
- Fulfilling social activities
- Creative expression – hobbies
- Meditation – contemplation
- Routine for domestic issues
- Freedom of expression – spirit

DEEP BREATHING

During stressful states we tend to adopt shallow breathing patterns, which compound problems by depriving the body of vital oxygen, and blocking the elimination of carbon dioxide and other waste products. The following exercise is simple and effective in reducing tension and curbing anxiety.

EXERCISE

Inhale with a deep slow breath. Feel your abdomen expanding, and hold the breath to the count of five. Exhale very slowly, emptying your lungs completely. Repeat until you feel a sense of calm.

MEDITATION FOR HEALTH AND INNER CALM

As I ascend to the higher spiritual realms, my worldly cares are being left behind in the mundane world. As I rise above the influence of earth's gravity, I feel lighter and lighter. My mind, body and spirit are infused with the pure healing white light of spirit. As I merge and become one with the beauty and tranquillity of the spiritual realms of eternity, I draw upon the power of my higher self for vibrant good health and abundance of energy, and trust in my soul's wisdom to live in the light of truth. Give thanks.

Much of your pain is self-chosen.
It is the bitter potion by which the
physician within you heals your sick self.
Therefore trust the physician, and drink
his remedy in silence and tranquillity:
For his hand, though heavy and hard, is
guided by the tender hand of the Unseen.

(Kahlil Gibran, 'The Prophet')

ACHIEVING HEALTH AND ONENESS

Support your decision to be healthy and full of vitality with an affirmation. Many people have been rewarded with positive results by using one of the most famous and simple affirmations by Emile Cové: 'Every day, in every way, I am getting better and better.'

Albert Einstein observed: 'Physical concepts are free creations of the human mind and not, however it may seem, uniquely determined by the external world.'

The Equilateral Cross Contained Within a Circle has been revered down the ages as a symbol of 'wholeness.' As we have seen earlier the form and shapes of sacred geometry remind us, in the spiritual sense, of 'home'. Just as circles, triangles and symbols with 'golden mean' ratios trigger memories programmed within us, the equilateral cross contained within a circle shown in Figure 8 is thought to set in motion a spontaneous healing through balance and alignment of energies.

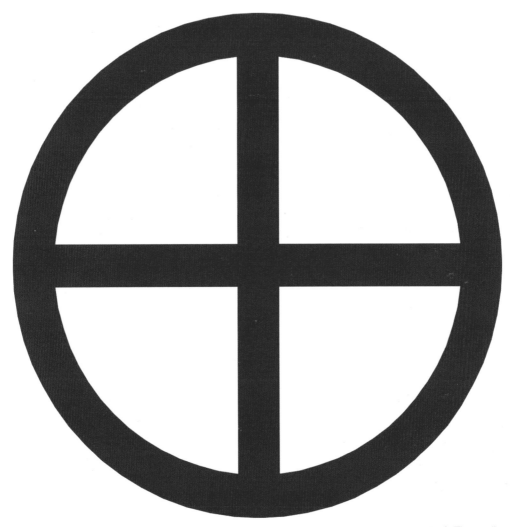

Fig 8: The equilateral cross
contained within a circle represents
a visual meditation for health and
oneness with all that exists

YOGA

Scientific investigations using advanced yoga practitioners have amply demonstrated that, through yoga, blood flow, skin temperature and the rhythm of the heart can be selectively regulated (see page 18). Therefore yoga techniques are used for survival in extreme cold and other physically and mentally adverse conditions. Yoga, like meditation, can disperse stress-producing hormones such as adrenaline, and promote hormones which have the opposite effect of promoting calm and well-being.

Healing Relationships by Mental Telepathy

*L*IGHT TRAVELS AT 186,000 miles per second; thought waves, which are electrical in nature, travel at infinitely greater speeds than light, which gives an indication of the power and effect thoughts can have on our lives, and the potential which they have to effect positive change on the planet. Mental telepathy is a powerful way of conveying reconciliatory thoughts and messages, in order to heal relationships. If attempts to heal a rift in a relationship have proved unsuccessful, positive thoughts sent with unconditional love can bring a 'change of heart' in the recipient.

Mental telepathy proved successful in the case of two sisters who had not communicated with each other since their father's death ten years earlier. Anne, the eldest sister, sensing that time was running out, desperately desired to make peace with her younger sister. Previous attempts had failed. Anne sat nightly in a relaxed meditative state, gently explaining to her sister that she wanted them to put the past behind them, and to transcend their differences. She visualized opening her heart and sending a stream of unconditional love. After one week, Anne received a letter in kind from her younger sister, explaining her compelling desire to reunite, which they then joyfully did.

In telepathy, as with any form of non-verbal communication or therapy, the integrity and wishes of the individual and their right to move on must always be fully respected. If after a reasonable time, say one week, there is no response, then accept that you have done the best you can, and if it feels appropriate do the affirmation of 'letting go' (see page 47). Many people have found that through the process of letting go the dynamics of the situation change, and a new sense of freedom paves the way to bring about a reconciliation.

The mind resembles a radio station, because it receives and transmits thoughts from many sources. The following story of monkeys on a small island off the coast of Japan demonstrates how information is disseminated around the world within like species, and when shared by a certain percentage of individuals can then become a universal reality. The monkeys had been observed by scientists for over 20 years. The monkeys ate sweet potatoes which they dug up, eating them along with the attached soil and dirt. One day, one of the monkeys carried a potato down to the sea and washed it in the water; gradually this was copied by more and more of the monkeys on the island, until the number reached around 100. Within one hour, scientists on other islands reported that the monkeys on their islands had also had acquired the habit of washing potatoes. This story also gives an example of the incredible power of our thoughts.

I had wonderful confirmation of the power of non-verbal communication with Henry, the resident cat where I was once staying. Henry appeared to have given up on life; for the previous few weeks he had stayed indoors sleeping on a shelf on top of a radiator, rarely venturing outside, and eating no food, although there were no signs of illness. Every morning I sat next to him eating breakfast, and telepathically I told him that he was healthy, loved and wanted. After three days we had eye contact. I then suggested that he would enjoy the garden and fresh air. Gradually the rare trips outdoors were extended and he started to eat again, taking an interest in his surroundings. After three weeks, Henry was fully restored to his old self.

SENDING MESSAGES

Choose a time when your mind is alert; your message will be clearer to receive if you keep it simple and gentle – it must never be coercive.

Sit in a meditative state. Request that the outcome of the communication be for the highest good of all those involved. Take a few minutes to energize your mind through deep breathing. The mind is electro-magnetic in nature, and will be invigorated by the life-giving oxygen distributed around the body via the lungs and bloodstream. Visualize the face of the person you wish to contact. Feel a stream of love radiating from your heart to the person. Start your message with their name. For example: 'Peter, I would like to end our hostilities and misunderstandings, and to renew our relationship in love and friendship. My message is sent with unconditional love.' Give thanks.

In formulating your message, check your motive to ensure that it is pure and unselfish.

A WAY OF BEING

There is a way of being
promoting love and selfless giving.

Not merely on the physical plane
but action in a spiritual vein.

Anonymous acts of generosity of spirit
seeking no recognition or personal merit.

Rich nourishment for the human soul,
aspirations of planetary health as its goal.

Receiving Help from the Higher Powers

RALPH WALDO EMERSON, in his essay 'Spiritual Laws', wrote: 'A little consideration of what takes place around us every day would show us that a higher law than that of our will regulates events.'

THE ETERNAL NOW

Past, present and future all exist simultaneously in what has been described as the 'eternal now', but their existence in different vibrational time-frames largely obscures them from our sight. Spiritual healers, shamans, mystics and creative people have managed to shift their consciousness to calibrate with these different time-frames and cross into other dimensions, in order to communicate with their ancestors' past lives and with geniuses, to seek guidance and wisdom. They have achieved this mainly through the altered, or non-ordinary, states of consciousness.

Precognition, in the form of warnings of impending danger, inspiration, healing diagnoses of illness and esoteric wisdom, has always been available through communication with the spiritual spheres. Mystic visionary and prophet Nostradamus (1503-66 AD) had an awesome gift for precognition; he predicted future events which he documented in annual almanacs. He accurately predicted the date of his own death, the Great Fire of London, the atomic bomb attacks on Nagasaki and Hiroshima, and named

Hitler in his prediction of the second world war. Many of his predictions named key figures and geographical locations of events thousands of years past his own time. In more recent times, world-renowned clairvoyant healer Edgar Cayce used his gift to help heal thousands of people in his lifetime; he also assisted in archaeological excavations in Egypt and elsewhere, using information from his clairvoyant readings.

The information received though visionary dreams, psychic reading and all other forms of 'channelling' often supply the answers by forwarding knowledge for the benefit of healing, science and the arts. Scientist Niels Bohr (1885-1962) was awarded the Nobel Prize for his work on the structure of the atom. He had received help through a visionary dream.

THOUGHT TRANSFERENCE

Mental mediumship and channelling, as it is also known, covers all aspects of thought transference, including mental telepathy on the physical plane between two or more people, communication with disincarnate beings, and contact with spirit guides and with the higher spiritual forces of the cosmos.

The twentieth century brought a proliferation of channelled writings, the origins being attributed to many sources such as spirit guides, ascendant masters and intelligences from other planets, such as the Pleiades. Jane Roberts, in her channelled 'Seth' books, offers this possible explanation for the origin of her work: 'Seth's books may be the product of another dimensional aspect of my own consciousness not focused in our reality.' She goes on to say: 'The funny thing is that a personality not focused in our reality can help people live in that world more effectively and joyfully by showing them that other realities also exist.' (From the book *The Nature of Personal Reality* © 1994, Jane Roberts. Reprinted by permission of Amber-Allen Publishing Inc., PO Box 6657, San Rafael, CA 94903. All rights reserved.)

Some of the great inventors, scientists and creative people in the arts and music now, in spirit, attempt to continue their work to assist us on the physical plane, helping to solve problems through visionary dreams, channelling and other forms of knowing. In 1970, a long-playing record of channelled classical piano music was released by Londoner Rosemary Brown, who had first been visited in spirit by Hungarian pianist and composer Franz Liszt as a child. In 1964, he reappeared and started to tutor Rosemary. Although a modest pianist herself, she managed to overcome technical difficulties and to commit the compositions to paper. Over the years she was visited by many of the great composers in spirit, including Beethoven, Chopin and Debussy. When the record was released, many famous musicians of that time expressed respect for the quality of the compositions, and their faithfulness to the individual styles of the great musicians. Rosemary Brown channelled an explanation from Sir Donald Tovey, a distinguished musician, also in spirit: 'The musicians who have departed from your world are attempting to establish a precept for humanity i.e. the physical death is a transition from one state of consciousness to another,

wherein one retains one's individuality.'

My own personal experience of channelled music followed a lecture by an alchemical hypnotherapist in California in 1988. In a past life, he had been a seventeenth-century court jester in France. Upon request, he demonstrated his musical skill in that lifetime. Going into an altered state of consciousness, he performed a 15-minute recital of seventeenth-century piano music, all the more impressive as he could neither read nor play the piano in this lifetime. The court jester was possibly another dimensional aspect of his own consciousness, focused in another reality.

Pierre Teilhard de Chardin stated: 'We are not human beings having a spiritual experience – we are spiritual beings having a human experience.' This tends to confirm that seeking to receiving help and guidance from the spiritual dimensions is as natural an activity for human beings as contacting each other on the physical plane.

CONTACTING SPIRIT GUIDES AND PAST-LIFE PERSONALITIES

After completing this exercise, your requests and questions will have been received by the higher spheres, and may be answered at a later time through means such as visionary dreams.

EXERCISE

Clear all the energies in your meditation space with a pure white light. Take time to go into a meditative state. State your intention to meet with your spirit guide or a past-life personality. Always have a clear pure and unselfish motive; ensure that your motive resonates in harmony with your integrity and is only for the highest good.

Visualize yourself in a safe place, a beautiful room, a glorious sunny beach or walking along a woodland path. When a figure appears, ask 'Are you living in the light?' If the answer is not an immediate 'Yes', then firmly tell the figure to leave. When you receive an immediate 'Yes', then ask, 'What is the message or information which you wish to tell me?' Request clarity if you do not fully understand. When asking your questions, be as clear and specific as possible, dealing with one issue at a time. Give thanks.

CONTACTING GENIUSES

The thoughts transmitted by our minds are electromagnetic in nature, and as such they attract other thought forces like themselves in our three-dimensional world, and as described earlier they travel at speeds infinitely faster than the speed of light, extending into the spiritual dimensions and beyond.

Start by making a serious study of the life and work of the genius whose mind you wish to attract. Read biographies and glean as much information about them and their life as you can. If the genius was a musician or composer, listen to their music; or, if an artist, make a study of their techniques to align your vibrations to resonate with theirs.

EXERCISE

When you feel you are ready, follow the previous exercise for contacting spirit guides. Having reached the state where you have visualized yourself in a safe place, request your higher self to contact the thought form of the genius. State your reason for the contact, making sure that it is clear and precise. Wait to receive a contact. As with any form of mediumship or channelling, always ask 'Are you living in the light?' Ask one clear question at a time, and again information may be received at a later time. Give thanks.

Countering Negativity

NEGATIVITY CAN MANIFEST itself in many ways, including feelings such as a desire for revenge, problems with troubled disembodied spirits that are seemingly unable to move on, and psychic attacks. It is always better to adopt a positive approach, and try to counteract such negativity, rather than to feed and perpetuate it.

FINDING A BETTER WAY THAN REVENGE

Harbouring thoughts of revenge and bearing grudges anchors us firmly in the past, clouding our vision of the future. To move on, these thought patterns will eventually have to be released. Sending negative thoughts is a form of psychic attack, and seeking revenge is said to return to the sender tenfold. Retribution has been known to be swift via the boomerang effect. We cannot be all-knowing and have a total understanding of every set of circumstances that occurs in our lives, or have an understanding of their cause. Misjudgements and misunderstandings can be irrevocable and costly on all levels.

Always try diplomacy first. If that has failed, the following affirmation lifts matters above the human domain and places it within the higher realms of cosmic intelligence. Request that your actions be for the highest good of everyone involved.

EXERCISE

I am placing my problem in the hands of the higher realms of spirit. I am removing my mental energy from it, so that it may be resolved by the higher cosmic consciousness in accordance with the integrity of all involved, and resonate in harmony with the greater plan for this earth. Give thanks.

VENDETTAS

'Old sins cast long shadows' (proverb). Vendettas are revenge for family honour. In blood feuds, it becomes the duty of a relative of the murdered person to avenge the death by killing the murderer or one of his relations. Retaliation can be carried on down through the generations.

Harbouring negative thoughts and disseminating them through family and friends has the effect of perpetuating negative energies, which also casts a cloud over someone else's life.

You are not my enemies, you are my brothers and sisters.
You did not do anything to me or my people. All that happened a long time ago in the lives of our ancestors. And, at

*that time I might actually have been on
the other side.*

*We are all children of the Great Spirit,
we all belong to Mother Earth. Our
planet is in great trouble and if we keep
carrying old grudges and do not work
together, we will all die.*

(Chief Seattle)

COSMIC ENERGIES

*Cosmic Guiding Intelligence
flowing through eternity*

*Felt, as rhythms of the invisible;
Heard, as music of the spheres*

*Highest consciousness permeating life
faithful to the universal laws*

*Source of wisdom and inspiration
cause of overwhelming amazement*

*Earth bathed in the Cosmic Light
People power to use its might*

RESCUE WORK WITH DISEMBODIED SPIRITS

Rooms or areas where the energies feel very
dense or turbulent can be caused by recent
events, or events that happened way in the past.
Occasionally a disembodied spirit fails to move
on to the higher levels, not realizing that they
have passed into spirit, or they are held back by
an overwhelming desire to complete a task in the
physical world.

If you sense that there is a 'presence' in an area,
use the following rescue work exercise. The exercise performs an invaluable service not only for
the disembodied spirit but also for the energies of
the earth. A strong attachment between a living
person on our physical plane with a person who
has died and passed to the spiritual realms affects
the spiritual journeys of both parties, neither being
able to move forward. (No harm will come in the
event of there being no disembodied spirit there.)

EXERCISE

Stand in the middle of the area. Take a few
breaths and relax. Request protection and
guidance from the spirits of light. Focus
your attention and request that the
outcome be for the highest good of all
involved. Ask for the appropriate spirit
helpers, living and working in the light, to
come and assist to liberate the disembodied spirit by guiding it to its rightful home.
Take time to repeat the request three
times. Give thanks, and blessings.

The Chinese have understood the value of clearing energies and creating sacred sites for thousands of years, through the ancient art of Feng
Shui. Practitioners were consulted in the search
for the most auspicious building site for the new
home, and also the most advantageous position-
ing of the rooms. Emphasis was placed on creating a harmonious and balanced environment
though the correct flow of energy).

If you would prefer to have help with rescue work, there are many consultants who clear energies. Feng Shui and psychic rescue workers can be located through the 'Resource Directories' of spiritual and metaphysical magazines. Esoteric bookshops and crystal shops usually have good networking systems, and can be a fund of valuable information. If you are thinking of a housewarming present for yourself or friends, a house clearing and balancing could be a very charming and beneficial present, as well as an auspicious start to a new life cycle.

BLOCKING PSYCHIC ATTACK

Psychic attacks usually manifest as negative thought patterns, originating from envy, jealousy, anger or thoughts of revenge being transmitted from one person's mind to the perceived cause of the negative feeling, most often another person. The power of the mind projects thoughts faster than the speed of light, and often it is not realized that by having these thoughts and connecting them to another person is actually the same as transmitting them, and they will be received at some level of the psyche.

That is bad enough, but an organized psychic attack, performed with intent to harm, is obviously totally against the universal spiritual laws. If you sense that you are the subject of an attack, take positive action to protect yourself. Cease thinking and talking about it, or visualizing the person or persons involved; this stops fuelling it with your precious energy. Affirm that you are taking charge of the situation and not becoming a victim. Cleanse your aura with the violet flame exercises on page 33.

If you find difficulty in blocking out unwelcome thoughts and images, visualize pulling down a heavy blind to conceal them. This will programme your mind not to accept them. If you sense that obsession is involved in the situation, make an affirmation to return all thoughts which are not yours back to their source. Protect yourself by putting a silver cage around you, and request that your spirit guides place you in the light. Affirm that you will live your life fully and joyously. Give thanks.

Spiritual Prenatal Care

*I*N HIS BOOK *The Psychology of Childbirth*, Dr A. Macfarlane tells us that 'a thousand years ago there were prenatal clinics in China, not so much in the interests of physical well-being as to ensure the tranquillity of the mother and, through her, of the baby'. Today ultrasound scans have shown that the unborn baby is sensitive to touch and sound and responds to external stimuli, such as doors banging loudly. Professor A.W. Liley explains that it has been known that the unborn baby moves rhythmically to certain kinds of music.

During sessions in hypnotherapy and rebirthing, clients have experienced waves of positive energies bathing their bodies, and feelings of warmth and love, while in the womb. Conversely, negative feelings will also be registered. Many people have known, for example, that they were not the preferred gender before birth. Research has shown that the baby in utero uses quite elaborate perceptual processes.

For many years now, setting up a mother-baby dialogue during pregnancy has been widely used. The following story is an example where 'telling the baby what is happening and reassuring it' would have been very valuable.

Ben was in a rebirthing session. He had not previously known that his birth had been surgically induced because he was overdue. This was later confirmed by his mother. This is how he described his experiences in the womb: 'To my horror, I became aware of a shining sharp metal object coming directly towards my face. A wave of absolute terror swept through my whole body.' A few days after the session, Ben realized that he had lost his unaccountable fear of being struck in the face, which he had since birth.

This is the heart-warming story of Anita, a home-birth midwife in America. One of her clients had decided to have her second baby at home, her first having been delivered by Caesarean section. The second birth made good progress, until a similar point was reached where the Caesarean section was required during the birth of the first baby. Around this time, Anita's friend, also a midwife, rang to ask how things were progressing. After having the situation explained to her, the friend offered to come and help, bringing along another friend who was also a midwife. The three midwives then held hands and meditated over the mother and baby. The birthing started again, and the baby was born quickly with no further intervention.

Most cultures aspire to rites of passage to assist their children through life's journey, such as baptism and bar mitzvah. These rites of passage are treated with the utmost respect and a high value is placed upon them.

Frederic Le Boyer believes that the birth experience leaves a deep and lasting imprint on the adult. Now that there is evidence that the baby in the womb is far more aware than had been previously supposed, why not have a rite of passage *in utero* and at the birth – the journey from the womb to the world – welcoming the baby and offering love and support? Offering the reassurance that the baby will be accepted as a unique individual with their own soul journey being recognized as a paramount consideration. If there has been a rejection of the baby on some level early on in the pregnancy, it might be possible to redress the balance by asking for understanding and forgiveness.

As with therapy on adults, it is important not to invade boundaries. The uterus is the boundary of the baby. Seek permission before starting any therapy, such as massage. This shows a respect of the rights of the individual within the boundary. A tranquil mother creates a tranquil child.

TWENTY-FIVE
MEDITATIONS

ENERGY SERIES

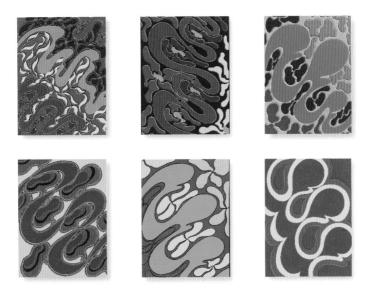

PULSE

LINK TO THE BEAT OF THE EARTH, THE BEAT OF NATURE.

Earth is the home of our three-dimensional body. We can be healed, revitalized and protected by the pulsating beat of energy flowing from the centre of the earth. When mind and body are receptive and in harmony with the earth's flow, it brings stability and joy of inner peace through the radiant flow of the life enhancing energy.

TAKE TIME TO ENJOY THE RADIANCE
OF NATURE'S ENERGY

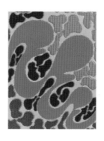

VERVE

SENSE THE VITALITY IN ALL LIVING THINGS

An inexhaustible flow of vital energy is constantly available to us through positive intention. Life lived with enthusiasm and vigour attracts these energies in abundance, bringing inspiration and stamina to enrich our personal experience of life. Verve, positive intention and enthusiasm enjoy their own vital energy and magic.

FOCUS YOUR AWARENESS ON THE POWER AND MAGIC OF POSITIVE INTENTION

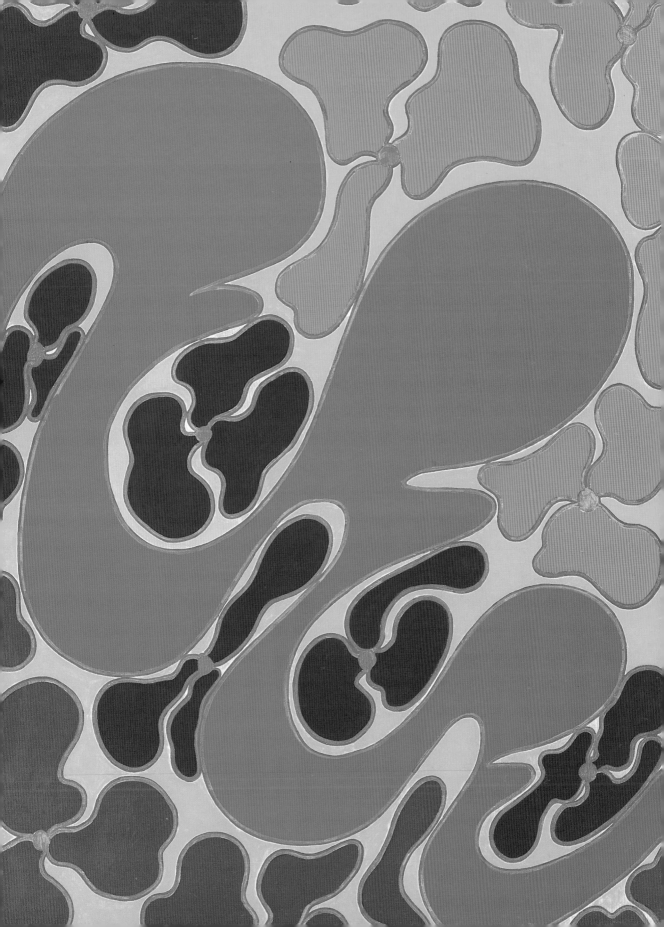

HARMONY

HARMONIZE WITH ALL THINGS

Our essence, the core energy of our being, is part of the interconnectedness of all living things on earth, the cosmos and beyond. All life strives towards a natural state of harmony, through personal awareness and intention. We are able to resonate in harmony with the cycles of universal energy, and live harmoniously in relationship with all things.

LET YOUR CORE ENERGY SLOWLY RADIATE OUTWARDS
TO RESONATE WITH THE UNIVERSAL ENERGY
OF ALL THAT IS

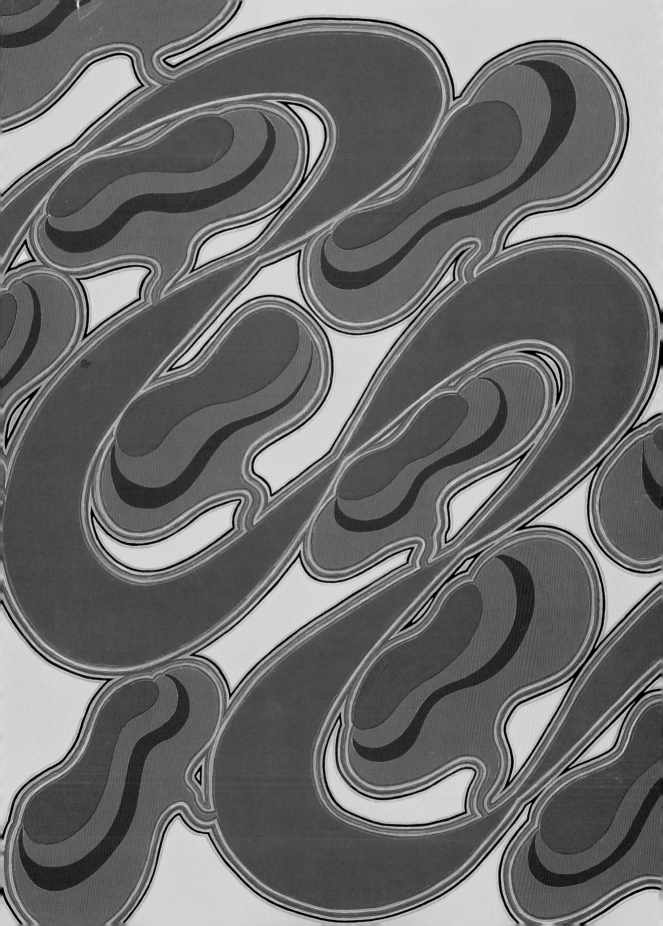

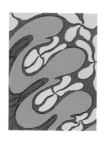

SYNCHRONICITY

ENJOY SYNCHRONICITY THROUGH INNER PEACE

A flow of vital information circulates within the collective unconscious and Cosmic Consciousness, which gravitates naturally to like minds and interests. When the mind is in a state of inner calm, it is open to receiving this information and to connect the patterns of the mind with the patterns of matter, resulting in a synchronicity of events in our physical world. Synchronicity also enables our consciousness to resonate in harmony with the changing vibrations of the earth, bringing us to a deeper unity and understanding.

LET THE ENERGY PATTERNS OF YOUR CONSCIOUS MIND
CONNECT AND BE IN HARMONY WITH
THE ENERGY PATTERNS OF MATTER

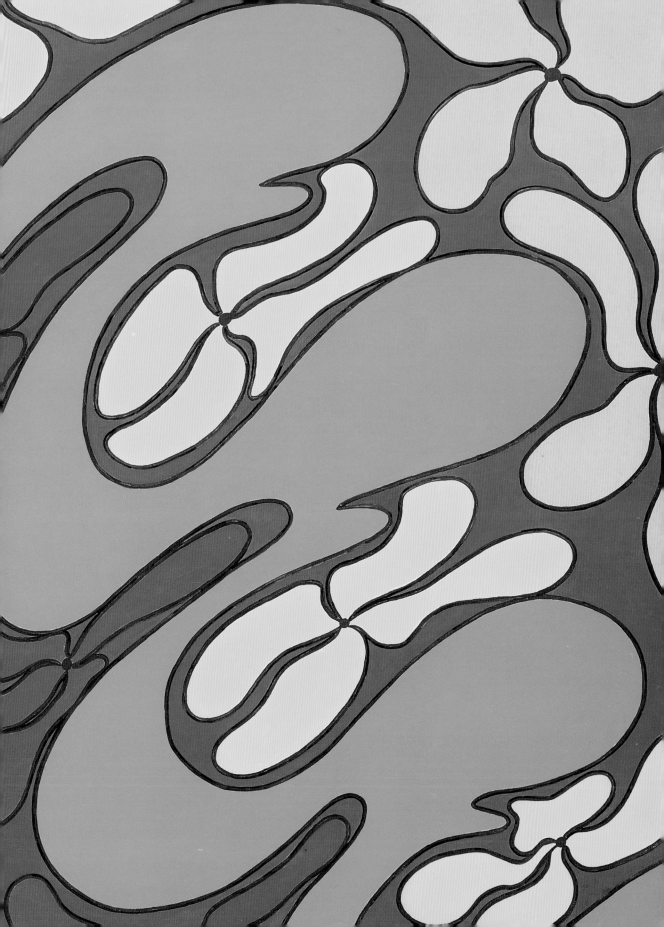

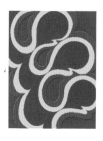

PERCEPTION

LOOK THROUGH EYES UNCLOUDED BY DOUBTS

In the absence of doubts caused by negative emotions, the mind's
perception becomes crystal clear, recognizing the truth through the
soul's integrity and intuitive knowing. Clear perception and awareness
go hand in hand, and clear perception allows for vision to travel
beyond first sight, towards awareness of the higher planes
of cosmic consciousness.

ENJOY THE BEAUTY AND SIMPLICITY OF CLEAR
PERCEPTION THROUGH THE SOUL'S INTEGRITY

CELLULAR SERIES

FUSION

BLEND WITH LIFE'S FLOW

Our energy and the energy of all living things originates from the same source and are constantly interacting. By blending with life's flow in a positive way, and treading a path of equilibrium in life, we heighten our own vibrations to resonate in harmony with nature, and contribute to heightening the earth's vibrations towards moving into the light.

BLEND WITH LIFE'S FLOW TO EXPERIENCE
THE LIGHTNESS OF BEING

TRANSMISSION

OPEN CHANNELS FOR COMMUNICATION

Wisdom, inspiration and healing vibrations are accessible to us all through physical and mental channels. When we are in a state of balance the chakras readily receive, assimilate and distribute the subtle energies throughout our system. The energies can originate within the mental, emotional and physical body, from the pure energy of nature, from the collective unconscious or from the cosmic rays, all of which are considered paramount to 'wholeness'.

OPEN MENTAL AND PHYSICAL CHANNELS TO RECEIVE
WISDOM, INSPIRATION AND HEALING VIBRATIONS

PERSPICACITY

CULTIVATE SIMPLICITY FOR CLARITY OF MIND

Simplicity and clarity of mind assists in the effortless flow of internal and external information which is received and interpreted into meaningful form, to be utilized for the highest good of the whole self. Cultivating simplicity by sincerity of purpose and intention sits comfortably with our highest integrity and conveys clear uncluttered messages for the mind to process.

VISUALIZE YOUR MIND BEING CRYSTAL CLEAR AND THE THOUGHT ENERGIES FLOWING EFFORTLESSLY

SURRENDER

TRUST IN THE HIGHER PLAN

The ebb and flow of life is regulated naturally, by the principle of alternating effort and relaxation and spontaneous natural changes. Trusting and accepting changes with a recognition of life on earth as a learning-ground for the spirit enables us to ride the highs and lows of life with equanimity and inner security.

TAKE TIME TO CONTEMPLATE ADVERSITY AS BEING AN OPPORTUNITY FOR SPIRITUAL PROGRESS

PROFUSION

REJOICE IN EARTH'S PROFUSION

Our physical world mirrors our thoughts, desires and expectations. It is though the quality of our thoughts and inner desires, that our physical reality is created. When we recognize and rejoice in the earth's rich resources, we are able to enhance the quality of our life, drawing upon nature's abundance and profusion.

TAKE TIME TO RECOGNIZE AND REJOICE IN NATURE'S PROFUSION

COSMIC SERIES

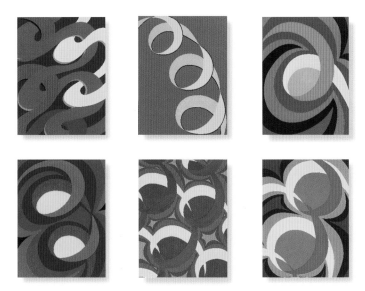

EMPATHY

SEEK TO UNDERSTAND OTHERS

Listening and observing with a silent mind, free of pre conceived ideas and prejudice, liberates our mind to focus on the positive aspects of others, and to recognize and enjoy their aesthetic qualities. Our thoughts and images, which we send out in silent communication, can be a direct return flow of empathetic energy which encourages full expression of ideas, the first step to fulfilling dreams and visions. We in turn expand our own consciousness through understanding and the experience of others.

LIBERATE YOUR MIND BY SEEING AND HEARING WITH A SILENT MIND

EXPANSION

DEVELOP AWARENESS BY PERCEPTION

When a point of balance exists in a calm, clear mind, it is possible for us to perceive the world perfectly through a heightened sense of awareness. The mind can then faithfully translate and process impressions and messages of guidance and wisdom from internal and external sources received through the chakras and senses.

EXPERIENCE YOUR MIND AS A POINT OF BALANCE AND HEIGHTENED AWARENESS THROUGH CALMNESS AND CLARITY OF PERCEPTION

PRE-EMINENCE

SEE THE ONENESS IN ALL THINGS.

We are made up of the same energy as all matter forming the universe and, as such, we are part of the interconnectedness of all living things and inanimate objects which form the earth and everything within it. The underlying principle of our spiritual experience is life as a state of balance and harmony within the oneness of the universe, our mind, body and spirit being aspects of that same oneness.

BATHE IN THE LIGHT OF ONENESS, LETTING
IT ILLUMINATE YOUR BEING

FIDELITY

BELIEVE IN YOUR INTEGRITY

Being true to our integrity is the key to fidelity towards our wholeness and soul's purpose. Our personal integrity is our standard of judgement in all aspects of life. Actions, ideas and beliefs that resonate in harmony, and sit well within our integrity, are touchstones to our highest authentic truth within. They are beacons of light on the journey through life.

EXPERIENCE YOUR INTEGRITY AS A GUIDING LIGHT
ILLUMINATING YOUR PATH

WHOLENESS

INTERACT WITH NON-ATTACHMENT

When we reach a state of interacting with non-attachment and
honesty within ourselves, our true nature emerges through clarity of
inner being, allowing life to be lived to the full. By refusing anything
which is not authentic to our true essential nature, and letting go of
imaginary images of ourselves, the self is unified into wholeness.
We can then enjoy freedom without being tied to anything
or anyone for our sense of identity.

ENJOY THE FREEDOM OF LIVING IN YOUR
TRUE ESSENTIAL NATURE

PERFECTION

HAVE FAITH IN THE GREATER PURPOSE

We come into this world endowed with our own gifts and talents, and with a blue print of our potential to guide us on our personal journey through life. Trusting in our own destiny with awareness, and holding faith in the greater purpose brings inner peace and security. Trusting in the grace of our being by living to our natural rhythms, and doing the best we can in all circumstances, is perfection.

CELEBRATE LIFE WITH COURAGE TO TRULY BE YOURSELF HAVING FAITH IN THE GREATER PURPOSE OF LIFE

GALACTIC SERIES

OMNIPOTENCE

RESONATE WITH THE UNIVERSAL MIND

We are capable of emitting and receiving energies of very high frequency. Life and optimum health rely on the balance of all our energies and the balance and harmony of the many energies which we absorb and which affect each other. When our energies are in their natural rhythm, it is possible to open a connection from our higher self to unite with the higher realms of thought field, progressing to resonate in harmony with the cosmic universal mind, leading us to higher levels of being.

OPEN CONNECTIONS FROM YOUR HIGHER SELF TO UNITE WITH THE COSMIC UNIVERSAL MIND

GENEROSITY

GIVE FROM THE SOUL WITH A GENEROUS SPIRIT

Giving from the soul in the true spirit of wisdom and love is also a gift to ourselves. When generosity originates from our inner vision and honest intention, it can not only support, heal and uplift the recipient, but also greatly enrich our own lives. Generosity of spirit, as with all good actions, generates positive vibrations which permeate all etheric space, having beneficial effects on the world of matter.

CONTEMPLATE YOUR GENEROSITY ORIGINATING FROM YOUR INNER VISION

BENEVOLENCE

BATHE ALL DECISIONS AND ACTIONS IN THE LIGHT OF BENEVOLENCE

When the connection to our higher self is open, and we are living in step with the higher qualities of life, our decisions and actions reflect the powerful forces of higher wisdom and understanding. Interacting with generosity of spirit increases our ability to reflect the light of the soul. In the interdependence of all life, our actions in the service to others, ultimately, give help to the planet by the generation of light.

EXPERIENCE YOUR ACTIONS AS A REFLECTION OF THE LIGHT OF YOUR SOUL

ALTRUISM

ENJOY THE NATURAL GIFT OF CONCERN FOR OTHERS

Observing events and circumstances with an open heart promotes deep understanding and sensitivity to the needs of others. Through this heightened sense of awareness and natural gift of concern, we are in the position to help others to discover and manifest their potential, and by so doing we can also discover and move closer to manifesting our own.

OPEN YOUR HEART TO EXPRESSIONS OF
UNCONDITIONAL LOVE IN UNDERSTANDING
AND CONCERN FOR OTHERS

FORGIVENESS

THE REWARD FOR FORGIVENESS IS MOVING FORWARD

Forgiveness of ourselves and of others in the process of letting go of
the past, clears and purifies the mind. It creates a subtle energy field,
releasing trapped negative emotions. An inner environment is created
in which unconditional love and creativity can manifest can flourish.
Every life experience we encounter however adverse, can be used as an
opportunity towards self knowledge and awakening, moving us
ever forward to the higher aspects of being.

ENJOY LIBERATION AND A FREE SPIRIT, THROUGH
RELEASING THE PAST AND FORGIVENESS
OF YOURSELF AND OTHERS

INFINITY

REJOICE IN THE CONTINUITY OF SPIRIT

Death is a transitional state, through which our spirit and soul transcends to the non-physical realms of spirit, which is as natural as our life in the physical world, being an integral part of nature. Just as we gravitate to beings who resonate in harmony with us in the physical world, we gravitate to spiritual beings with the same vibrations in the non-physical realms, always existing within the totality of all life.

EXPAND YOUR CONSCIOUSNESS TO EXPERIENCE THE TOTALITY OF ALL LIFE AND CONTINUITY OF SPIRIT

ETERNITY

CELEBRATE IN THE GRACE AND ILLUMINATION OF ETERNITY

Eternity lies in the present, with past, present and future being contained within the 'eternal now'. It is within the present that our point of power is anchored in the moment. In meditation and dreams we glimpse our spiritual home in the cosmic realms of eternity, revealing infinite lifetimes transcending time and earthly limitations, strengthening our sense of oneness with the eternal cosmic whole.

BATHE IN THE RADIATION'S OF PURE LIGHT AND GRACE OF ETERNITY, AND LET IT ILLUMINATE YOUR PATH THROUGH LIFE

Living to our true nature

THE FRENCH PHILOSOPHER La Rochefoucauld wrote: 'We assume the look and appearance we want to be known for, so that the entire world is a mass of masks'. Living with grace and ease in one's own true nature generates inner peace, spontaneous natural joy, good health and a freedom from fear.

'Know thyself' has been a recommendation towards awareness and enlightenment from ancient times. Socrates echoed this advice when he pointed out that: 'Man's basic error lies in ignorance of his true nature'.

Discovering true nature and experiencing our pure essence involves the mind, body and spirit working ceaselessly in order to resonate harmonically with universal rhythms. In the tranquillity of the meditative states, one is able to discern the deep, natural rhythms within the self – and able to the synergy between personal, life-based, deep natural patterns and those which are universal. They are replicated throughout all existence and we experience them in the changing of the seasons, phases of the moon and even in our own breathing in and out.

Goethe stated: 'Man seeks his inward unity, but his real progress on the path depends upon his capacity to refrain from distorting reality in accordance with his desires'. So often, a crucial incident becomes the catalyst for revelation and change, bringing us closer to our true nature. An example is that of personal loss- where the death or other forfeiture of a loved one – when reflection and reconsideration of past decisions and attains can be seen as having been only in the consideration of the relationship, and never simply as a fulfilment of ones own, direct wishes. Through such misunderstandings of self, or actions which we seem to undertake simply to keep the peace', it is all too possible that we enter into a false way of being without any realisation of that state. Real life situations should be as fair and equitable as is possible, with a conscious balancing of all relevant considerations.

For example, children often adopt mechanisms involving different personas for coping with, and negotiating, the obstacles of life. Tailoring these to suit stressful situations, such attitudes can be perpetuated into adulthood, concealing the true self. Changes can the only occur when a conscious and decisive plan of action is formulated. Such a decision needs clarity of purpose, even a dream or vision, and be capable of being carried through to fruition with real passion and enthusiasm.

If life seems like an endless boxing match, against a perfectly matched opponent, each round following interminably and without result it is hard then not to recognise that the opponent is actually yourself.

When all is said
And all is done
It matters not
Whom is deemed to have won

What matters most
Above all else
Is how one, finally,
Views the self

Further Reading

Bailey, Alice A ., 1953: *Esoteric Healing*. New York: Lucis. 1960: *The Rays and the Initiations*. New York: Lucis.

Blair, Lawrence,. 1975: *Rhythms of Vision*. London: Croom Helm.

Cambell, Joseph., 1993: *Myths to Live By* .U.S.A. Arcana.

Capra, F., 1982: *The Turning Point*. London: Fontana.

Costenada, Carlos., 1993: *Tales of Power*. U.S.A. Arcana.

Cunningham, Donna, and Ramer, Andrew, 1988: *The Spiritual Dimensions of Healing Addictions*. San Rafael, CA: Cassandra Press.

Ferguson, Marilyn., 1981: *The Aquarian Conspiracy*. London: Routledge & Kegan Paul.

Genero, Luigi, and Guzzon, Fulvio, and Marsigli, Pier Luigi., 1980: *Kirlian Photography*. London: East-West Publications, U.K. Ltd.,

Gerber, Richard., 1988: *Vibrational Medicine*. Santa Fe: Bear and Co.

Grof, Christina and Stanislav., 1991: *The Stormy Search for The Self*. London: Thorsons.

Haich, Elisabeth., 1965: *Initiation*. London: George Allen and Unwin.

Harris, Thomas., 1970: *I'm OK -You're OK*. London: Jonathan Cape.

Heath, Robin., 1999: *Sun, Moon and Earth*. Powys, Wales: Wooden Books.

Kubler-Ross, Elizabeth., 1975: *Death: The Final State of Growth*. New York: Prentice-Hall.

Lopsang Jivenah (ed.), 1995: *The Life of Milarepa*. UK: Llanerob Publishing.

Macfarlane, A., 1977: *The Psychology of Childbirth*. U.S.A: Harvard University Press.

Martineau, John., 1996: *Mazes and Labyrinths in Geat Britain*. Powys. Wales: Wooden Books.

Ouspensky, P.D., 1988: *In Search of The Miraculous*. U.S.A. Arcana.

Oyle, Irving., 1975: *The Healing Mind*. Millbrae, C.A. Celestial Arts.

Roberts, Jane: 1994: *The Nature of Personal Reality*. San Rafael, CA: Amber-Allen.

Sheely, Gail, 1977: *Passages*. London: Bantam.

Simonton, Carl., 1978: *Getting Well Again*. U.S.A: J.P. Tarcher, Inc.

Glossary

ALCHEMY – mythical art of turning base metal into gold.

AURA (auric energy field) – the area of activity in the atmosphere surrounding the body.

CLAIRAUDIENCE – the ability to hear things at a subtle level, not normally perceptible to the senses.

CLAIRVOYANCE – the ability to see things not normally perceptible to the senses. Also known as second sight.

COSMIC CONSCIOUSNESS – the Essenes conceived of the whole universe as a cosmic ocean of life, in which currents of cosmic power are continually uniting all forms of life on all planets and connecting humans with all other organisms (from 'The Teachings of the Essenes').

COSMIC RAYS – radiation of great penetrating power, entering the earth from outer space.

COSMOS – the ordered universe.

DIVINATION – the ability to foretell the future.

ESOTERIC – arising from within.

ESSENE – member of an ancient Jewish esoteric order, started in the Middle East in the first 200 years AD.

HIGHER SELF (or higher consciousness) – operates at levels above the conscious mind, with higher-dimensional powers and principles, and unaffected by social and environmental considerations.

HOLISTIC – derived from the Greek *holos* (whole), this refers to an understanding of reality in terms of the integrated whole of mind, body, emotions and spirit, all affecting each other, and not being separate from the interconnectedness of everything.

INCARNATE BEING – in the flesh, living being.

INTEGRITY – our own personal standard of judgement.

LAW OF CORRESPONDENCES – sometimes known as the principle of 'as above so below'.

MANTRA (yantra) – invoking a spiritual, emotional and mental harmony with the universe.

MENTAL MEDIUMSHIP – includes all communications, from telepathy between people in the physical world to contact with beings in spirit, to the higher spiritual forces in the cosmos.

MERIDIAN SYSTEM – forms the physical-etheric interface.

METAMORPHOSIS – a change of form or structure, evolution.

PERSPICACITY – quick mental insight.

PRECOGNITION – previous knowledge.

SUBCONSCIOUS MIND – operates below the conscious mind; our waking experiences are stored there.

SYNCHRONICITY – the acausal connections between imagination and thoughts in our internal world and events in the external reality.

TOUCHSTONE – used for testing the purity of gold and silver.

Index

I wo ed me
to us , and
Robi g and
maki

M 7, San
Rafae rsonal
Realit es.

I g ll the
autho

My copy-
editor so to
George Sharp and Richard Carr for their design work on the book.

Very special thanks go to my son Ben, who did the additional
drawings, and to my son Sam, who photographed the original
illustrations, and his partner Miranda, all of whom generously gave
their continuous encouragement and support.